SEO Consultant Spills His Secrets: Discover How To Rank Higher, Outsource To The Right SEO Service Provider And Take Advantage Of FREE Search Engine Traffic

Sam Adodra

SEO Expert Strategies

SEO Consultant Spills His Secrets: Discover How To Rank Higher, Outsource To The Right SEO Service Provider And Take Advantage Of FREE Search Engine Traffic

Limit Of Liability / Disclaimer Of Warranty:

This book was diligently researched and compiled with the intent to provide information for those wishing to learn about Search Engine Optimisation (SEO) and find out what is working today to help improve their search engine rankings.

Every effort has been made to ensure the highest amount of accuracy and effectiveness. The author does not however warrant that the information contained within this book is free of omissions, errors or is fully complete.

The publisher and author specifically disclaim any implied warranties of merchantability or fitness for a particular purpose and make no guarantees that you will achieve any particular result.

The publisher and author expressly disclaims any liability arising from any strategies, techniques, services and advice provided in this book and shall not be held responsible for any damage or loss alleged to be caused or caused indirectly or directly by this book.

All content, products and services are not to be considered as legal or professional advice and are to be used for information purposes only. Any services offered within this book are provided on a best efforts basis.

The purpose of this book is to educate and guide and the advice herein may not be suitable for your own situation. The author recommends that you carry out your own due diligence.

Any brand names or product names mentioned in this book are trademarks or registered trademarks of their respective companies.

Any reference to an organisation or website in this work as a citation and/or potential source of information does not imply that the publisher or author endorses the organisation or website.

Further, readers should be aware that Internet websites listed in this work may have changed or disappeared after this work was written.

Read This First

- Thank you for purchasing SEO Expert Strategies -

You will get the most value from this book if you download the Audio Book and the Cheat Sheets action guide. They are both 100% FREE.

1. Read the main book: SEO Expert Strategies

2. Listen to the accompanying Audio Book

3. Go through the Cheat Sheets action guide

Download your bonuses from:

http://www.SamAdodra.com/audio-book

Acknowledgements

There were so many people that inspired me to write this book.

I am grateful to every person that has entered my life, even those that I only shared a brief conversation with. Whether the experience was good or bad, you have in one form or another helped to shape my vision for the future.

To my family and friends: thank you for your ongoing support and encouragement. I value your presence in my life. You have helped me to become the person that I am today.

I also acknowledge the numerous coaches that have openly shared their wisdom, success stories and numerous failures. You have made me realise the importance of giving back and helping others in their journey.

There were several people that helped me to refine my ideas and make this book come to life: Chandler Bolt, James Roper, Tyler Wagner, Chris Winters, Neil Patel, Ana Hoffman and Lise Cartwright.

Thank you for helping me to stay positive, focussed and making this book something that I feel proud to share.

Table of Contents

A Note To The Reader

Thank you for purchasing this book.

My name is Sam Adodra and I am a Search Engine Optimisation (SEO) consultant. If you want to know more about me and my services then you can find out by visiting http://www.seoservicelondon.org

This book is primarily aimed at SEO professionals at an intermediate and expert level. I recognise however that some readers may be at a beginner level and for this reason I have included a section on how to get started with your own link building.

If you are an owner of your own business and currently outsource your SEO, this book will equip you with the knowledge of what your SEO professional is (or should be) currently doing to help improve your rankings.

If you are a busy business owner with no passion for learning how to improve your website rankings or whose time is scarce, then it may be in your best interests to pass this book onto your marketing agency or SEO consultant.

Search Engine Optimisation is a huge subject that could be taught as a degree in its own right. Learning SEO is a skill that can take months or years to master.

In addition, a good SEO professional needs to regularly test to keep up with the numerous algorithm updates that have come out in the past few years.

This book is a good foundation for those that do not have the time or resources to carry out their own testing. This book is not however, and was never intended to be, an ultimate guide encompassing all of the information related to SEO.

If I attempted to write a comprehensive guide about SEO then it would quickly be out of date by the time that it was brought to market. In 2014 there were 13 major algorithm updates and hundreds of minor ones from Google alone.

As an SEO professional, I want information that is on the cutting edge, not what was working 12 months ago.

The primary aim of this book is to provide you with the latest strategies so that you know where to focus your SEO efforts, hence the emphasis on today's top ranking factors.

This book has been compiled based on copious testing using data collected from over a thousand websites, from different owners across the world. I do not guarantee that your results will be the same as ours.

There are so many variables in SEO, from receiving an over optimisation penalty to picking up links from a 'bad neighbourhood', that can affect your rankings.

A site registered as new may in fact have previous history that you are not aware of. Before purchasing a domain you should carry out research.

If you have a number of websites, on different hosting accounts, then you are more likely to see common themes in your rankings than with just a single website on a shared hosting account.

Having multiple websites on different hosting gives you the flexibility to test different variables and an opportunity to compare your research with ours.

If you find any differences then I invite you to contact me on 020 8938 3645.

In summary, this book provides information on where you should be focussing your SEO efforts to get the maximum benefit, i.e. the highest rankings.

The SEO industry is extremely fast moving and I advise you to put these methods into practise immediately. Alternatively you can just give this book to whomever you are currently outsourcing your SEO to.

They should be able to interpret the information within this book and understand it much better.

If you do not have an SEO professional and are looking for one then you may be interested in our 'done for you' service.

Availability in the 'done for you' is intentionally limited because I personally work with you and do not wish to compromise the quality of service.

Depending on when you contact us there may be a waiting list.

Details about the service are available near the end of this book in the 'Next Action Steps' section.

Chapter 1

What Is SEO (Search Engine Optimisation)?

1. Introduction

SEO (Search Engine Optimisation) encompasses the use of techniques to help a website rank higher in the organic search results. The organic search results show up in the non-paid section.

The objective of SEO is to improve visibility by showing up high in the search results. This helps to bring targeted traffic to your website. Generally the higher your website ranks the more visitors you will receive that are looking for your product or service.

What people type into the search box of the search engines, i.e. the search phrase, is commonly referred to as a keyword. With the organic search results there is no cost for the website owner when a user clicks on their website.

Traffic sent to your website from Google, Yahoo or Bing (or any of the other search engines) is therefore free.

SEO falls within the broader topic of Search Engine Marketing (SEM). SEM is a term used to cover all marketing strategies for search and includes both organic and paid searches.

2. Paid vs. Organic Traffic

Paid search works on a bidding scale process. The more you bid for your ad to show, the higher your website will be in the paid ads section of the search results as long as the ad is relevant, i.e. congruent with your website content.

Going down the paid route means paying every time that a user clicks on your ad, irrespective of whether or not they purchase from you. Traffic sent in this way is not free. With paid ads you can specify a daily budget so that once the budget is exhausted your ad will no longer show.

The search engines are strict on what content can be displayed in the ads and where a user is taken when they click on an ad. The search engines require paid ads to pass filters before they are approved.

After approval, the position in which the ad shows up is influenced by budget and other factors like the copy in the ad, user click through rate and whether the ad landing page complies with the search engine's terms of service.

There is a general consensus amongst search engine marketers that consumers trust the organic search results over the paid search results. Consumers understand that the search engines rank on merit and a website that has an organic listing on page one is there because it's earned.

In contrast, a website that appears in the paid ads section is there because the owners have paid money to be listed. A savvy consumer may question if the website that appears in the paid ads section will still be there tomorrow.

3. Benefits Of SEO

It is important for your business website to be listed in the search engines because consumers across the globe conduct several hundred thousand searches every single second, and this is just in Google, the biggest search engine.

If your website is not listed in the search engines then you can be sure that your competition already is and are already benefiting from free traffic that the search engines are sending them.

The focus of this book is on SEO, i.e. the ability to rank in the organic search listings and the major emphasis is on Google because it is the largest search engine. The majority of search traffic across the world flows through Google.

On August 16th 2013 between 6:52pm and 6:57pm EST (Eastern Standard Time), Google experienced a rare failure. This meant that if you went to Google.com you could not access Google's website.

Every other website on the Internet was still running, including the other search engines, Yahoo and Bing. The likes of Facebook, YouTube, Twitter, Amazon and all other sites were still live and could be accessed by going directly to those websites.

In the 5 minutes that Google was down, traffic across the globe fell by a massive 40%.

Focussing on search engine traffic can be a huge factor in bringing targeted traffic to your business website. With the recent explosion in mobile, including smartphone and tablet growth, getting online has never been easier.

Today, consumers rarely look in printed media like the Yellow Pages, the telephone directory or a newspaper. Instead, they do a quick 'Google search' on their smartphone or PC.

What does this mean for you? If you want to get in front of your customers then you need to be visible when they search for your services or products. You can achieve this with a strong online presence.

Google is the online equivalent to all of your printed media so it makes sense to get found in the world's largest search engine. A big advantage of search engine traffic is that it's targeted. This means that your website will only be shown to consumers that type in specific search phrases (keywords).

Ranking for a bunch of related keywords makes sense because not every single customer types in exactly the same keyword even if they are looking for similar results.

The main objective of the search engines is to return relevant results to the end user. If the user's needs are met, they will be a happy searcher and will likely return the next time they need to search for something.

If the user does not find what they are looking for then they may switch to an alternative search engine.

4. How Search Engines Work

Before a search engine can display relevant results to an end user it needs to archive the information that is available on the web. This is achieved by small pieces of software commonly referred to as 'spiders' that crawl the web by scanning for content and following links.

These results are then returned to the main 'bot'. A bot (web robot) is a program that runs automated applications over the Internet. Google's bot indexes results from the spiders and uses proprietary methods to rank the websites for particular results (keywords) that end users search for.

The proprietary methods used to rank these search results are collectively known as the algorithm. The search engines do not make all of the factors that go into their algorithm public knowledge. If they released this information then it would be possible for anyone to work their way to the top of the search results.

An SEO professional will attempt to reverse engineer the algorithm by taking the information that is available and combining it with their own testing to find out what works. The proof lies in whether a website ultimately climbs in rankings or drops.

In recent years there have been a large number of algorithm updates. This means that many SEO practices that worked a year ago may no longer work today. The main purpose of this book is to share with SEO professionals what is currently working.

5. Indexing

If a website is not indexed then it will not show up in the search results. Unless your website has engaged in shady business tactics, for example trying to cheat its way to the top of the search results, then it is likely that your website is already indexed in all of the major search engines.

However, you may have content (inner pages) on your website that does not get indexed by the search engines. This can be done either through choice, i.e. you insert a specific piece of code that tells the spiders not to crawl a specific page, or it could be because the page could not be found by the spiders.

Linking to that page, either by internal website links or through external websites will usually help the spiders to find that page and index it.

The major search engines are constantly indexing hundreds of millions of web pages. They determine what is shown in the SERPs (search engine results pages) when you enter a search query by looking broadly at two main areas. These two areas are discussed further in Chapter 3. In brief they are:

1. The content on your website – this is referred to as 'On Page SEO'

2. Who is linking to your website – this is referred to as 'Off Page SEO'.

6. Different Search Results

If the same search is carried out across different search engines, it is likely that you will see different results.

The reasons for this are because each search engine uses a proprietary algorithm which applies different weighting factors to determine what results show up in their result pages when a search query is entered.

Since Google is the dominant search engine across the globe it makes sense to focus your efforts on them.

An authority site that ranks well in Google generally tends to rank well in Yahoo and Bing too. This is because most of the important factors relating to On Page and Off Page SEO will already have been adhered to if your website ranks well in Google.

Another way of looking at this is to view Google as the quality control.

Depending on which country you are based in, the traffic that flows through Google is typically anything between 64-90% of all search engine queries.

"...view Google as the quality control"

Chapter 1 Summary

Key Takeaways

In Chapter 1 you learnt the following:

1. What is SEO (Search Engine Optimisation)?

2. The difference between organic and paid traffic and which type of traffic consumers trust more.

3. The benefits of SEO for your business and how much global traffic passes through Google.

4. How the search engines index content from across the web to rank in the SERPs.

5. The difference between On Page and Off Page SEO.

6. Why search results differ between the major search engines and why Google should be viewed as the quality control.

What To Expect In Chapter 2

In the next chapter we'll discover why Google is committed to refreshing its algorithm with regular updates and how this is good news for those of us that want to build our brand ethically, using White Hat SEO methods.

Chapter 2

Introduction To The Animals: Panda And Penguin

1. Panda

Google has released two major updates to its algorithms in recent years. The first was called Panda and this was released in February 2011.

Panda's objective was to reduce the number of lower quality sites, for example sites with only a single page or just a few pages, and push higher quality sites nearer to the top of the SERPs.

In doing so, Google were able to clear up spam caused by 'content farms' that released both low quality and duplicate content.

Many sites prior to 2011 had been using spammy, Black Hat techniques (e.g. keyword stuffing the page and creating thousands of backlinks through software tools) to rank 'thin sites' near the top of the SERPs and cash in through advertising, e.g. with Google Adsense.

Since 2011, there have been numerous updates to Panda. The 24th version (Panda #24) arrived on January 22, 2013.

In 2013 there were an additional 3 updates to Panda: Panda #25 on March 14, 2013 and Panda Dance on June 11, 2013. On July 18, 2013 came Panda Recovery.

The most recent Panda update was released on May 20, 2014 and was officially named by Google as Panda 4.0 - meaning that most of the previous updates were iterations upon the major Panda updates.

Panda 4.1

Panda 4.1 was released on September 23, 2014. According to Google, approximately 3-5% of search queries were affected.

The update enabled Google to focus more precisely on the identification of low quality content.

User feedback to Panda 4.1 was generally positive as it allowed small and medium sites of high quality to gain a boost in the SERPs.

2. Penguin

Google's second major algorithm update was first announced on April 24, 2012. Penguin was brought in to deal with Black Hat SEO techniques like:

a. Keyword stuffing

b. Cloaking (where search engines see one thing and visitors see another e.g. making certain text the same colour as the background so that it is invisible to the user but will get picked up by the search engines)

On May 25, 2012, Google released another Penguin update, called Penguin 1.1.

The main purpose of the update was to penalise websites using manipulative techniques, usually with the help of software, to achieve artificially high rankings.

Whilst Google claimed that the update was meant to catch excessive spammers, it also appeared to affect legitimate sites and SEOs.

Successive updates to Penguin have been brought in since. In 2013, big updates to Penguin were released with version #4 (referred to by Google as Penguin 2.0) released on May 22, 2013 and the most recent version #5 (referred to by Google as Penguin 2.1) released on October 4, 2013.

The most recent updates to Penguin appear to have focused on over optimisation of anchor text.

Although Google releases several hundred updates to its algorithms each year, the majority of these are tweaks.

With Panda and Penguin, a major shakeup occurred in the SERPs.

When Google releases an update to Panda or Penguin, it is common for some sites to jump or drop tens or hundreds of positions if Google finds something about your site that it likes or dislikes.

The older way of doing SEO (even up till 2012) is having considerably less effect and today may even no longer work.

Google regularly refreshes its algorithms to help deal with spam and return relevant results to its end users. If you want to rank your website today then you need to be wary of any SEO firms that still engage in Black Hat SEO techniques.

The safest way to future proof your website from new updates is to build authority to your site.

This can be achieved by increasing the amount of quality content that you release and engaging more on your social media profiles to help bring traffic back to your website and pick up 'natural links'.

These are techniques that Google refers to as 'White Hat SEO'.

Penguin 3.0 & Everflux

Penguin 3.0 was released on October 17, 2014. This update was less drastic than Penguin 2.1 and was to be a "refresh" according to Google.

The update was estimated to affect less than 1% of all US English search queries.

The update was of benefit to users that had fixed their bad backlink profiles but which had not recovered from Penguin 2.1.

On December 10, 2014 Google released Penguin Everflux. A Google representative said that Penguin had shifted to continuous updates, moving away from infrequent, major updates.

Chapter 2 Summary

Key Takeaways

In Chapter 2 you learnt the following:

1. The two major algorithm updates released by Google in 2011 and 2012: Panda and Penguin, and the objectives behind each release.

2. Why Google is regularly refreshing its algorithms and how to future proof your website from these updates.

3. Why older methods of doing SEO are having less impact and may no longer work today.

What To Expect In Chapter 3

In the next chapter we'll be going into detail on how to set up your website structure correctly. This will provide Google with the information it is looking for.

Following these steps will give you a competitive advantage and build a strong foundation for your SEO campaigns.

We'll also introduce Off Page SEO and learn how to find quality links that will propel you high up the SERPs.

Chapter 3

Explanation: How SEO Works

1. Introduction

SEO comprises both:

    a. On Page - the content on your website and how it is arranged

    b. Off Page - who links to your website

In order to rank well, you only need to be better optimised than your competition. In a low competition market it is possible to rank a website with good On Page SEO only.

The more competitive your market place, the more you will need to rely on Off Page SEO to help you rank.

The information presented in the following pages is based upon several studies on websites in the UK and the US. I have pooled data from my own results and also included tests from my peers and from Search Metrics results.

For reference, the results shown have been accumulated from over a thousand websites, each with a different class C i.p. address and hosted on different servers.

2. On Page SEO

On Page SEO is defined by the multiple elements on your website that are in your control and that can be changed. Optimising the following will make it easier for the search engines to index your content and understand what your website is about.

i. Content

Always use original content. Using somebody else's content is not only plagiarism and unethical but can land you with a potential penalty. If you struggle to create your own content then you can pay for others to create it for you.

The web has a number of article writing services where you can pay writers and claim the rights to the content as your own.

If your website attracts a lot of visitors, e.g. to your blog, I suggest that you re-write a purchased article in your own words so that your readers get accustomed to your style of writing.

In previous years it was possible for a person to submit an article to their blog and have someone else scrape the article and rank higher with this duplicate content.

The result is that no one would know who the original author was. Most people would assume that the higher ranking website was responsible for creating the content and unfairly give them the credit, e.g. by referencing on social media.

To combat this Google introduced 'authorship'. This is where the owner of a website (or the author of an article) creates a Google Plus profile to let Google know that they are the contributor towards a particular website.

Google then recognises who the author of the content on that website is.

Google uses a number of ways to verify ownership of the website. An easy way to verify ownership is to take the html code that Google provides and upload it to your website, e.g. by placing it in the header section so that the code appears on every single page of your website.

Once Google has verified ownership it will crawl your website when new content is created.

As long as your content is original you will be recognised as the author of the content even if it later gets scraped by another user.

A former benefit of authorship was the ability to have a thumbnail image show up next to your website in the search engine result pages (SERPs). However, on June 25, 2014, Google announced that it would be removing this benefit.

John Mueller, Webmaster Trends Analyst at Google, provided the following explanation in a post on his Google Plus profile:

"We've been doing lots of work to clean up the visual design of our search results, in particular creating a better mobile experience and a more consistent design across devices.

As a part of this, we're simplifying the way authorship is shown in mobile and desktop search results, removing the profile photo and circle count."

A thumbnail image in the SERPs attracts attention because our eyes are naturally drawn towards images. This type of 'rich snippet' image helps a website to stand out and increases the click through rate and conversion.

There is a general consensus in the SEO industry that Google actually removed thumbnail images from the SERPs because it was affecting the CTR (click through rate) on its paid ads.

Despite this recent change, I am still of the opinion that authorship has many benefits. Authorship provides a trust signal for your website and some website owners even claim that it provides a small ranking boost.

I have not included authorship as a confirmed ranking factor though because of the lack of data.

When you post your content, I recommend that you focus on your readers and not try to optimise your content for the search engines.

It has been a common practice for marketers to bold, italicise and underline specific keywords. This practice no longer carries any weight and may put off your readers.

Instead you should create content that your audience will find engaging and valuable.

Google has become adept at words that are related (synonyms) and so if your content is natural and flows, you can expect to build authority with Google by increasing the trust that it has in your website.

Building authority should be the ultimate aim of a website owner if you want to maintain long term rankings. As you build authority you also create more trust in Google.

You will then find it easier to rank for more general keywords, related to your content, without the need to build backlinks.

ii. URL Structure

Some content management systems, for example WordPress, create inner pages using a system of arbitrary numbers. The url for a new page looks like:

http://www.mydomain.com/p156

This makes the task of the search engines more difficult because /p156 does not mean anything.

What you actually want to do is set up your urls so that they have your keywords as part of the inner page url.

If you wanted to rank for the keyword 'dog training specialist' then your url should look like:

http://www.mydomain.com/dog-training-specialist

Having your keyword in the url can help to give you a ranking boost because the search engines understand the url structure better.

In WordPress you can change the default settings using the permalinks tab which is under settings and then select custom structure.

In the box enter /%postname%/ to ensure that when you create a new post or page, it is automatically named according to the title that you give the article.

iii. Pictures

When you conduct a search online what stands out in the search results? Videos stand out because they have a thumbnail image attached to them.

A website can stand out by using rich snippets, e.g. gold star review ratings.

We humans are visual creatures. Our eyes get drawn towards images more easily than text. As the saying goes, a picture says a thousand words.

Use images to draw your reader in to your content.

A picture is also a great way to break up sections of text.

Using a picture can also help the search engines to identify what the content on your web page is about providing you label the images correctly.

You can do this by naming the file of the image with one of your keywords. So instead of using pic568.jpg, use something like 'dog-training-manual.jpg' or anything that is related to your keyword and that also describes the image well.

Using the alt tag function to attach text to the image can help with your On Page SEO because you can put an extra keyword in here.

Remember, the search engines are not humans. They cannot see images like we can so they rely on meta data like tags, description and the file name to interpret what the image is about.

It's always best to use your own images on a web page but if you are stuck then you can search for royalty free images and purchase images for your own use.

I strongly recommend that you do not use other people's images without permission. This includes going to Google images and searching for something in your niche.

Many images have tags which can help the image to be traced back to the original source.

In the past few years there has been a significant increase in the amount of copyright infringements. Law firms that specialise in copyright can get access to sophisticated software that scans the Internet for a plagiarised image.

Using someone else's images without permission could land you with a hefty fine of several thousand pounds/dollars.

iv. Title Tags & Meta Tags

Every web page has a title tag with a text headline. The text that appears at the very top of your web browser is the title tag.

Title Tags: the text that appears at the very top of a web browser

Title tags have a maximum of 75 characters so choose your text carefully. Put your main keyword in but do not keyword stuff or over optimise.

The title tag appears as a blue link in the SERPs:

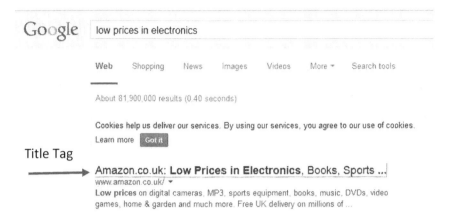

Meta tags are snippets of code that can be used within a web page's html. There are two meta tags: meta description and meta keywords. The meta description is the text that describes what the web page is about.

This text is included in the description part underneath your url in the SERPs. The following image shows a search for 'low prices in electronics'.

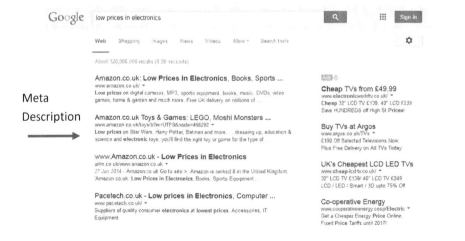

Amazon's meta description is:

'Low prices on digital cameras, MP3, sports equipment, books, music, DVDs, video games, home & garden and much more. Free UK delivery on millions of ...'

The meta description is an opportunity for you to use engaging text that will help a user to click on your website.

If you do not include a meta description then the search engines randomly select 150 characters of text from your web page content instead.

The meta keywords provide an opportunity to list some additional keywords that relate to your web page.

In the early days of the Internet the search engines used meta keywords to help identify what your website was about.

In 2009, Google released a notice specifying that meta keywords were no longer part of their algorithm. This is largely down to the potential to 'keyword stuff' this section.

Bing is known to go one step further. They see meta keywords as a potential spam signal and if you include them but do not subsequently use these keywords in your content then your site may be penalised.

Some of the smaller search engines still use meta keywords so it's your call whether to include them.

v. Header Tags

The information in the header tags such as <h1>, <h2> and <h3> is treated as a title by the search engines.

Including your keywords in these tags can help the search engines to scan your web page and understand the content.

Your main keyword, i.e. the one that gets the most searches, should go in the <h1> tag. The other tags, <h2> and <h3>, carry less weight so include your smaller keywords only if they naturally fit.

You can check that your page has been indexed by doing a search for the title of your page using "..." a few days after you have published your content.

If the title of your page was: Dog Training Course For Beginners In London then you would search for "dog training course for beginners in london" into the search bar.

Where exactly you rank will be determined by the number of competing pages.

Placing your title in "..." indicates that you want an exact search for this long tail keyword (your title) so it should show up on the first page if the page has been indexed, assuming that other websites have not got an identical title.

Using header tags also makes it easier for your reader to digest your content as it breaks up the text into bite size chunks.

Bounce rate is becoming an important factor in other search engines determining how relevant your site is to an end user.

The longer you can keep a user on your web page the more beneficial it will be for your longer term rankings.

vi. Internal Linking

Internal linking is the process of cross referencing material from one page to another page on the same website. Link juice flows through all the internal links. Wikipedia.org is a good example of a website that uses internal linking well.

Setting up internal links from the home page to inner pages can be very powerful once your domain starts to build authority.

This is how large sites often appear at the top of the SERPs for smaller keywords without having any backlinks built to their inner pages.

The search engines treat internal links just like a backlink from an external website. Before you start creating lots of internal links on your website I recommend that you speak to an SEO professional.

It is very easy to over optimise your anchor text and get hit with a penalty.

A big advantage of internal linking is the potential to keep a user on the website for longer. It's common for a user to land on the home page and then scroll down looking for more information if they find the content useful.

Having internal links within your content can help the user to reach your inner pages more easily.

The more a user engages with your content, the more likely they are to convert to your products or service.

3. Off Page SEO

i. Introduction

Off Page SEO is defined by all the activities that are outside the boundaries of a website. Off Page SEO is given more weight by the search engines than On Page SEO because it is a measure of how much importance others give to your website.

It is important to remember that the search engines are robots. They do not interpret websites like humans and cannot make an informed decision about how good a website is based on its design, layout and quality of the content.

A search engine instead relies on signals like how many links are pointing to that website, where the links are coming from (as an indication of quality of link) and how often that website is talked about on social media platforms.

A link that points from one website to another is referred to as a backlink. Several years ago the search engines ranked websites based on how many backlinks pointed towards it.

This strategy quickly became abused as Black Hat SEOs began to artificially build links with the help of software and promote their sites to the top of the SERPs.

In the past few years, Google and the other major search engines have made a big effort to clean up the SERPs by placing more weight on the quality of a link.

The process started with Google allocating a level of authority called Page Rank (PR) to every website on the Internet.

Sites with high authority - i.e. those which have a high number of naturally acquired links, a large amount of pages and a strong level of user interaction tend to acquire Page Rank more quickly than smaller websites.

Google is keen to steer Internet users away from Page Rank as a metric of quality but it is still commonly used by SEO professionals to gauge authority.

A website with a PR4 is regarded as a higher authority than a website with a PR1 score.

The rest of this section introduces the different ways to create a link and explains the difference between a good link and a bad link.

Off Page SEO is covered in more detail in the following chapters.

ii. Anchor Text

Anchor text is the text used in a blue hyperlink when one web page links to another web page. If you have an internal link going from your home page to an inner page then you might use an anchor text like click here to direct your visitor to the inner page.

A website that links to yours is like a vote of confidence signal for the search engines. If a keyword is used in the anchor text, e.g. red balloons this tells the search engines that your site is about red balloons.

The search engines then scan the rest of your content on the web page to see if there is anything related to red balloons. If there is content about red balloons, the incoming link is deemed relevant.

Building relevant links can increase the authority of a website and help it to rank higher for the keyword phrase in the anchor text. The search engines also look at the content on the site that is providing the link as an indication of how relevant the link is.

iii. What Makes A Good Link?

A good link is one that comes from a high authority domain in your own niche. If a website is ranking on the first page of the search engines and has been there for some time (i.e. not just appeared for a few months and then disappeared in the next algorithm update) then you can safely assume it is seen as an authority.

The problem is finding a good reason for the authority site to link back to your site. What's in it for them? If your website is young then you probably need the authority site more than it needs you.

Building up a relationship with the owner of the authority website or connecting with the authors that write the content would be a good start.

In reality, this could take several months or even years and that's assuming they give you the time of day.

You could try to get a guest blog post on their website but the likelihood is that others will also be doing the same. An alternative route is to build up your own authority so that your status rises.

Once this happens, the authority website would see you as more of an equal and probably be more likely to engage in a conversation with you. Building authority does take time so it's a good idea to find out what else makes a good link.

As the search engine's algorithms become more sophisticated, understanding what makes a good link will give you an advantage in staying power.

With the shift towards quality over quantity, you should focus your efforts on finding higher quality links instead of chasing after lower quality links.

If a link is easy to get for you then it will also be easier for your competitors to get too.

The factors that contribute towards a quality link include:

    a. Authority

    b. Relevance

    c. Link Type

    d. Location Of The Link

    e. The Does It Feel Right Test

Each of these is covered in more detail below:

a. Authority

Whilst the ideal scenario is to get a link from a site in your own niche that is already ranking high on the first page of the search results, this isn't always practical.

You can still look for authority links from other countries or from a related niche and these will still count as quality links.

SEO professionals evaluate authority in different ways but there is a general consensus. An authority link combines Page Rank (Google's standard) with standards set by Moz: Page Authority (PA) and Domain Authority (DA).

Until recently, Google would regularly update Page Rank several times a year. Since 2013, Google has reduced the number of public Page Rank updates and this is why other metrics like a domain's age, page authority and domain authority are being used more frequently to evaluate overall authority.

The benefit of an authority link can be much greater than just the link juice it provides. A site that gets a link from an authority site will also receive new visitors and this effect is amplified if the link is on a high traffic page like the home page.

If you want to grab the attention of an authority site then you should make the effort to actively participate on their blog and leave intelligent comments that add value to the discussion.

Also make sure you to check out all of the social media platforms where they post to and actively contribute there too.

b. Relevance

The search engines want to provide the end user with a good experience and this is why they constantly update their algorithms to try and improve the SERPs.

Let's consider that you own a site in the dog training niche and a visitor lands on your website. They read your information and decide to click on your outbound links.

If you have a link to a technology blog then it's probably unlikely that the visitor will stay for long on the technology blog. The information isn't relevant to what he's looking for.

If however, you have a link to a website that sells pet food and your visitor clicks on that link, there is a higher chance of them staying on the next website for longer.

This is because the information is related to the content on your own site.

The search engines follow the links that you place on your website and they also see the links that come into your website.

If they determine that your inbound links are relevant, you will be rewarded with a higher ranking boost than if your inbound link is from an unrelated site.

Relevance is measured at both page level and domain level. Consider the previous example. An incoming link that is from a web page about dogs and where that same website is about dogs will be of high relevance.

An incoming link from a web page about dogs where the rest of the website is about sports will only be of partial relevance.

c. Link Type

There are different ways to create a link on a website. The most common type is the anchor text link.

I. Anchor Text Links

This is the visible, clickable part of the link that contains text.

If you are trying to rank for the keyword 'dog training specialist' then you should be getting a percentage of your links with the anchor text as 'dog training specialist'.

Be careful about getting too many links with the same anchor text. This will lead to an over optimisation penalty from Penguin.

II. Naked Url

This is the full url, i.e. http://www.mydomain.com. Using the full url as the hyperlink is seen as a very natural way of linking from one website to another. Since no keyword is used there is no direct ranking benefit from this type of link. There is also no risk of receiving an over optimisation penalty.

A site can still build up authority if all of the backlinks are naked urls (assuming that the links are DoFollow – i.e. link juice/authority is allowed to flow) but it will struggle to rank well for any major keywords because there is no information that tells the search engines what your site is about.

III. Image Link

This is when an image is placed on a web page and a hyperlink is created from the image to another url. If a user clicks on the image they are taken to a url that is in the hyperlink.

If you have a long article on a web page then you can use images to enhance the user's experience by hyperlinking the image to a different section on the web page.

For example, a hyperlink in an image at the bottom of a page could return a user to the top of that web page. This way the user could avoid having to manually scroll to the top of the page in their browser.

Another reason for hyperlinking an image to a different part of the same web page is when you have a direct call to action for the user, e.g. a buy now button or an opt in form where they enter their email address.

IV. Shortened Links

Shortened links (e.g. through http://bit.ly) are used to create easy redirects. This type of link is useful when you want a user to click on a long url.

Shortening the link could be for user convenience or to help cloak a link that looks spammy, e.g. an affiliate link.

Many platforms use shortened links. In YouTube for example, clicking on the 'Share' tab underneath a video presents a shortened link provided by YouTube for easy sharing on social media platforms.

Similarly, when you compose a message (tweet), Twitter will condense any urls in your message to help you squeeze more characters in.

V. Redirect Links

A redirected link carries little to no SEO benefit unless it is made through a permanent 301. A 301 redirect is when the authority of one website, built up through age and links, is passed onto another website.

A common reason for a business to use a permanent 301 redirect is when they setup a new domain and want to transfer all the benefits of their old domain to the new one.

Any traffic that lands on the old domain is automatically redirected to the new one.

It is worth noting that if an old domain has any search engine penalties, using a 301 permanent redirect will pass these penalties on to the new domain.

301 redirects can be created in the control panel of your domain hosting. If you want to redirect with a less permanent solution (e.g. for a specific event) then you can use the temporary 302 redirect link.

VI. No Follow and Do Follow Links

Having a blog with comments enabled can leave your website exposed to links from a 'bad neighbourhood'.

Enabling the comment feature is good for social proof and encouraging discussions on your blog but it also provides a user with the ability to get a link back to their own website.

This issue can be overcome by:

1. Restricting who can post a comment, e.g. by a user's i.p. address, limiting the number of comments made and manually approving all comments.

2. Installing a Facebook social plugin. This allows users who are logged into Facebook to add a comment to your blog.

   This is becoming a common feature on many websites with a blog as it adds a layer of social proof.

3. Disabling or closing the comment feature. Some blog posts continue to receive comments for months and years after the original post is made.

   Disabling the comment feature will deny your readers the opportunity to interact on your blog.

   A less drastic solution is to close the comment feature after a certain number of people have commented.

4. Making all links in the comment section No Follow. This last feature tells the search engines not to pass on link juice to the website of the person making the comment.

A blog with Do Follow enabled will attract visitors more easily than a blog with No Follow enabled. If your blog is new then you may want to start off with manually approving comments to avoid putting off your regular visitors.

d. Location Of The Link

Where a link is located determines how much link juice it passes on. In order of preference you should be aiming to get links:

1. In the main body content (this is referred to as a contextual link)

2. Underneath the main body content, e.g. in the biography box

3. In the sidebar

4. In the footer

Google interprets links in the footer as potential spam so ideally you should keep these to a minimum.

It is common practice for software (theme/plugin) developers to automatically place a link in the footer back to their main website when their theme or plugin is installed.

This was interpreted by Google as a deliberate attempt to game the system and they subsequently devalued the quality of footer links. Most people use the footer section for easy access to internal pages which is fine to do.

Do you need to be concerned if some of your inbound links are from the footer section of other websites?

Having a diverse range of links and even those from a different location is natural. A few links in the footer section will not hurt your site as long as you have a good variety of links coming from other locations.

e. The 'Feel Right' Test

Once you've mastered the above you should be in a good position to figure out whether a site is good to get a link from or whether you should give it a miss.

For example, a site that is relevant to your niche may have a large amount of outbound links (typically more than 50) in the comments section of an inner page.

In this case you may want to avoid posting a comment on that particular page. The search engines analyse the comments made above and below your own comment.

If your website is sandwiched between comments that link out to 'bad neighbourhood' sites, it could hurt your site.

Now, if you were the first or second person to comment on a site and that site subsequently gained a lot of traffic and attracted a lot of spam type comments, you may want to consider if it's worth posting to that site again in future.

If the blog owner is not regulating all the comments that are being made you could be putting yourself at risk.

On the other hand, if the comments are well regulated and the blog owner only approves intelligent comments, then you know that you are posting to a quality site.

With SEO, a general rule of thumb is to ask 'how hard is it for me to get this backlink?' If it's hard to achieve then you can assume that the quality of the link is high.

If the backlink is easy to get then it will probably have less value assigned to it by the search engines.

The purpose of blog commenting should be to leave a comment that adds value to the blog. This will help you to get the comment approved and also drive traffic back to your own website.

Having your comment approved also means an additional backlink to your site and this can help your rankings.

The 'Feel Right' Checklist:

1. How many outbound links are there on this page and also on the other pages on this website?

2. Are the comments well policed by the blog owner?

3. What is the quality of the content on the rest of the domain like?

4. How frequently is the blog getting updated?

5. Does the website have contact information (e.g. a contact form)?

6. Does the website have a social media presence (e.g. buttons linking to social media platforms) and is the website owner or blog post author active on social media?

Chapter 3 Summary

Key Takeaways

In Chapter 3 you learnt the following:

1. The difference between On Page SEO and Off Page SEO.

2. How to build trust for your website with Google authorship.

3. What a rich snippet is and why it can increase clicks and conversions.

4. The importance of structuring your website URLs correctly and making appropriate use of keywords.

5. The difference between title tags, header tags and the meta description and how these features display in the SERPs.

6. How internal linking can make it easier for the search engines to crawl and index your content and also for readers to access your inner pages.

7. The difference between a good link and a bad link.

What To Expect In Chapter 4

In the next chapter we'll learn about an excellent free tool for keyword research, how to find out which keywords your competitors are targeting and examine an untapped source of keywords for additional traffic.

We'll also cover how to use Google's own search function to help us find relevant sites in our niche for powerful backlinks.

Chapter 4

Getting Started With Your Own SEO

1. Keyword Research

Good SEO always starts with keyword research. Finding what keywords to rank for is critical as it provides the foundation to your SEO campaign.

If you get this part right then you could have a very profitable business. If you get the keyword research part wrong then you'll either end up ranking for keywords that aren't profitable, because there's not enough search volume, or you'll struggle to rank for the keywords you want to go after because the competition is too strong.

Google's free Keyword Planner is an excellent way to get keyword ideas. Type a broad keyword into the tool and it will provide you with a list of related keywords and how much search volume each keyword receives.

Keep in mind that the Keyword Planner is built for AdWords customers, not for SEO, so you should not rely on it to gauge the strength of your competition.

If you are new to a niche and not sure what keywords to target, research in the Keyword Planner and analyse the keywords that your competitors are targeting.

To find out your competitor keywords, add their url into the search box or landing page section of the Keyword Planner tool.

Google will return keyword ideas that it thinks are relevant to that particular site. You can then see how much traffic each of these keywords pulls in every month.

2. Checking How Competitive A Keyword Is

Understanding how many websites you'll be competing with for a specific keyword can give you an indication of how long it may take to rank.

The higher the number of competing websites, the more difficult the competition usually is.

Go to Google and type in the search string:

allintitle: "keyword"

Replace "keyword" with your own keyword phrase. Google will return the number of websites that have this keyword in the title of their website.

The number shown is how many sites are optimised for that particular keyword. If you are in a medium-high competition niche market it is important to check for synonyms of that keyword.

You can do this by using a thesaurus and also by looking at what other words Google bolds in the SERPs.

Anything bolded or highlighted is a word that Google interprets as interchangeable with the keyword that you type into the search box.

If you type 'Dog Training' into the search box in Google, you will also be shown results with 'Dog Trainers' in the website title.

A website can rank for a keyword even if it is not actively targeting that keyword, as long as a synonym of that keyword appears somewhere in the description (title, domain url or meta description).

If the keyword that you are hoping to rank for has lots of authority websites on the front page, each with high page rank and the keyword in the title of their website, it might take a while to get your website ranking.

In this situation you need to have a realistic expectation of whether you can compete for that keyword or whether it might be better to target a keyword with less competition.

In niches that get a high search volume, Google often provides a list of 'Searches related to' <your keyword> at the bottom of the SERPs. You can try going after one of these keywords.

If you are determined to go after a high competition keyword, make sure that you have the resources to match your competitors' efforts.

You should also factor in the time which your competitors have spent in building up the authority of their website.

Some factors to consider:

i. Does your website have some age to it (and therefore trust) or are you starting with a new domain?

ii. Does your website have any previous SEO history? An over optimisation penalty may hinder your chances of ranking.

iii. How well optimised is the On Page SEO of the sites that are currently ranking on page one?

iv. How many websites are you competing with? (allintitle: "keyword")

v. How strong is the domain authority of the sites currently on page one?

3. Additional Resources For Keyword Ideas

A resource less talked about is Google's suggestions. These are the phrases that Google offers when a user starts to enter their keywords into the search box. The suggestions provided are based on what has been previously typed in by other users.

The Keyword Planner does not include all of these suggestions. Using Google's search box to find all of the suggestions in your niche can be a slow process requiring trial and error.

It's likely that you'll end up missing a few suggestions even if you have the patience to use this method.

A better tool to find suggestions is http://ubersuggest.org.

Type in a keyword, e.g. dog training and select a language/country. From the second drop down menu select 'web' unless you want results for images or videos.

The first time that you perform a search you may have to enter a captcha.

http://ubersuggest.org

280 suggestions found.

Next, click on 'Suggest'.

The tool has found 280 suggestions and provides the most relevant results directly below your search.

⇧ dog training

- dog training
- dog training classes
- dog training courses
- dog training collars
- dog training leads
- dog training books
- dog training videos
- dog training jobs
- dog training equipment
- dog training glasgow

If any of these suggestions are relevant you can add them to your list of keyword ideas.

4. Introduction To Link Building

As the number of people using the Internet grows and more businesses come online, the competition to secure a first page ranking increases.

A decade ago it was possible to buy cheap traffic using Google Ads. Sending targeted traffic to your website could be done for just a few pennies.

Today, the cost of using Google Ads has rocketed, because of the number of people using the system.

A business with a small marketing budget has to spend very carefully on Google Ads and calculate if the cost of acquiring a customer through paid advertising is profitable.

The same holds true for SEO. Several years ago it was possible to put up a website with an exact match domain and rank on the first page just with good On Page optimisation.

Today, the algorithms for all of the major search engines are much smarter. On Page optimisation on its own is rarely enough to get you ranked, and keep you on the front page of the SERPs, unless you operate in a very low competition niche market.

The probability is that if you are in a niche that gets a decent amount of online search volume there will be competition. This means building links to your website using Off Page SEO.

To get started with link building we can use Google's search engine to find relevant websites in our niche that run a blog.

Most blogs have a section where it is possible to leave a comment. By leaving an intelligent comment with our name, email and website we can hopefully get the comment approved and in doing so build a link and get more traffic back to our website.

i. The Search Strings

Below are search strings that you can type into Google to identify sites to get a backlink from. The best sites are those in your niche market as these will count as 'relevant' links.

In the search strings below replace "add your keyword" with your own target keyword.

site:.com inurl:blog "post a comment" - "comments closed" -"you must be logged in" "ADD YOUR KEYWORD"

site:.gov inurl:blog "post a comment" - "comments closed" -"you must be logged in" "ADD YOUR KEYWORD"

site:.edu inurl:blog "post a comment" - "comments closed" -"you must be logged in" "ADD YOUR KEYWORD"

Explanation:

1. The 'site:.com' command asks Google to return searches for websites that have a .com ending. In the same way, site:.gov and site:.edu return searches for websites that have a .gov ending and a .edu ending.

These endings are referred to as top level domains (TLDs). In previous years, a backlink from a .gov or a .edu website was the gold standard for link building campaigns.

Government and university sites carry a significant weight in the search engines because they are viewed as high authority, trusted links. Having just a few of these could often propel a website onto the first page of the SERPs.

More recently, the ranking weight assigned to a .gov or .edu link has fallen but they are still seen as a trusted link, particularly if the link is relevant to your niche.

2. The 'inurl: blog' command asks Google to return searches for website that have a blog.

   Blogs are where an owner posts updates like new content and encourages interaction. Not all websites with a .com or .gov or .edu top level domain have a blog, so this part of the search string is asking Google to return results with sites that do have one.

3. "post a comment" command tells Google that you want it to return searches from sites that have a blog and that allow you to post a comment. Not all blogs provide an opportunity for a user to post a comment.

4. –"comments closed" is a negative search command. This command intentionally asks Google not to return results with blogs that have closed their comments.

   Some blog owners open their comments for a few days or only allow a certain number of comments to reduce the risk of spam on their blog.

5. –"you must be logged in" is another negative search command. This time we are asking Google to ignore results where a user has to be logged in to the website in order to leave a comment.

   Many .edu and .gov sites restrict commenting to internal users, e.g. students or employees to stop external users from posting on the blog.

6. "Add your keyword" command - you can replace the 3 words in quotes with your own keyword.

Example:

If you wanted to search for .com sites that are relevant to the weight loss niche, you would input the following search into Google:

> **site:.com inurl:blog "post a comment" -**
> **"comments closed" -"you must be logged in"**
> **"how to lose weight"**

Exclude A Specific Word

You can also tell Google to exclude a specific word from your search results. For example you may not want results that include 'how to lose weight slow'. In this case you add –slow. The search string then becomes:

> **site:.com inurl:blog "post a comment" -**
> **"comments closed" -"you must be logged in"**
> **"how to lose weight" -slow**

ii. The Google Dance

Some websites rank for long tail keywords without having any links built to them. This will be due to any of the following reasons:

1. Low competition

2. Good On Page optimisation

3. Keyword rich domain

4. Domain authority, e.g. aged domain

5. Brand trust, e.g. Google authorship, good presence on social media

When a website with no previous link building history suddenly starts to acquire links it may actually dip in the rankings. This is normal and is referred to as the 'Google Dance'. It does not mean that your website has incurred a penalty so there is no cause for panic!

If you start building links too quickly you may find that your website completely disappears from the SERPs. This does not mean it has been de-indexed. Instead, it means that you are building links too fast.

Slow down and you will find that your website returns within a few days or weeks.

With SEO, slow and steady wins the race. In a link building campaign it is normal for a website's ranking to dip and jump several places.

This fluctuation is part of Google's algorithm and occurs because there are so many factors that contribute towards the algorithm now.

A site can receive a boost for picking up a relevant link but then get hit by another part of the algorithm.

Once the link building campaign has finished, or the link building velocity has slowed down, your website will return to a stable position.

If the SEO has been done correctly your website should end up in a higher position than when you first started.

Chapter 4 Summary

Key Takeaways

In Chapter 4 you learnt the following:

1. The importance of keyword research for your SEO campaigns.

2. How to use Google to find the number of competing websites for any keyword.

3. A checklist to use before you target high competition keywords.

4. How to take advantage of Google's suggestion tool for additional keyword ideas.

5. Search strings that you can type into Google to help you find relevant websites for backlinks.

6. What the Google dance is and why it occurs.

What To Expect In Chapter 5

In the next chapter we'll go into more depth about On Page SEO factors.

You'll learn how to fine tune your On Page settings, without over optimising and how to get your content shared across different platforms on the Internet.

We'll also cover how to fix the holes in your website that leak out link juice and how to capitalise on a huge, growing traffic source: mobile

.

Chapter 5

Advanced On Page SEO

If you operate in a medium competition or high competition niche it is vital that you get the On Page foundation set up correctly. This chapter covers all of the important On Page factors in more depth to help you optimise your website correctly.

1. The Title

The html code of any website can be examined by viewing the page source. Enter the website url in the address bar and wait until the page has loaded. Then click the right mouse button and go to 'View Page Source'. To find out the title of your competitors' website search for the <title> ... </title> tags.

The title is like a book cover - it is a summary of your website. As it is one of the first lines of code that the search engines see, it carries a lot of importance.

You should include your brand name and/or your main keywords in this section to help the search engines understand what category or niche you are in.

If you're not sure what to put in the title it can help to examine your competition and get some ideas about what brand names or keywords they are using.

Go to Google (or the search engine that you normally use) and type a phrase into the search box. You can view the page source of the websites that appear on the first page of the search results.

The title of a website appears at the top of a browser:

For Amazon's website, their title reads: 'Amazon.co.uk: Low Prices in Electronics, Books, Sports Equipment & more'.

Amazon is a large, authority website that receives a huge amount of traffic. If we do a search for the first few words in Amazon's title, we should expect Amazon to appear near the top of the search results.

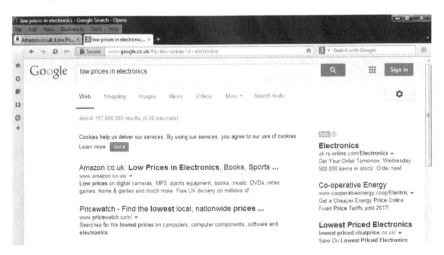

As we see, Amazon is in the number one spot for the search phrase 'low prices in electronics'.

What does this mean for you?

Placing a keyword near the beginning of your title can help your website to rank for that keyword if your website has authority. The title is an important factor in On Page optimisation.

However, Off Page SEO is more powerful than On Page SEO and so it is still possible for your competitors to rank for a keyword even if that keyword does not show up in their title tags.

Another reason for optimising your website title is the conversion element. Your website's title is what shows up in the blue text above your website url (see Amazon's example above).

When a user types a keyword phrase into the search bar, Google will bold any keywords that match the words in your title.

This helps a user to identify that your website is related to what they are looking for. This helps you pull in more targeted traffic and improves your click through rate.

Title optimisation checklist:

1. Keep the description to 60 characters or less. Any longer and the full title won't show up.

2. Put your main keyword at the beginning of the title where it has high priority. Google highlights keywords that match a user's search phrase so having your keywords at the beginning will help you to stand out.

If we examine Amazon's website again, a search for the phrase 'low prices in books' returns:

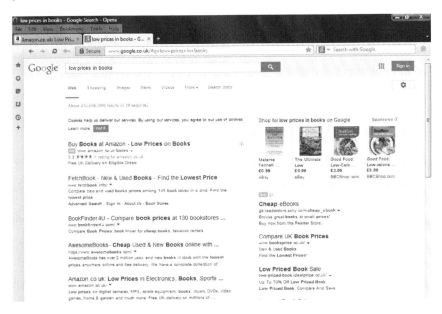

This time, Amazon is not ranked in the number one position for 'low prices in books' but instead is number four (excluding the paid ad at the top).

Google highlights the word 'books' because it matches the user's search phrase but gives preference to other sites that are more targeted to books. Note how the first three results have book in their domain url.

By contrast, Amazon is telling Google that it wants to give higher priority to the word 'Electronics' than it does to 'Books' based on the order of appearance in its title.

Amazon's authority means that it would likely rank in the number one position for 'low prices in books' if the title was re-arranged to position 'books' before 'electronics'.

3. The title is the one occasion where you have permission to optimise for the search engines and not users!

    Enhance your title by adding related keywords. This can help you show up for long tail phrases (search queries containing several words not just one or two). Make sure that additional keywords still make sense to the end user.

4. Do not keyword stuff here. You won't get any special preference and you may end up with a small over optimisation penalty.

5. Don't use special characters, like "@", "%", "!", etc. If you want to separate keywords use the character "|".

2. Headings

These are your H1, H2, H3, etc. tags. If you're not familiar with header tags, try analysing the page source for a popular blog in your niche. If you're in the dog training niche then search for 'dog training blog' and view the page source to find the <h1>, <h2> and <h3> tags.

After examining the title, the search engines look at the header tags to help identify what a web page is about. Header tags play an important role so where possible you should get your keywords, in order of priority, within these tags.

<h1> tag: Place your web page's title here (do not confuse this with the website title). The <h1> title should be keyword rich to help the search engines identify what your content is about, but make sure it reads well.

<h2> and <h3> tags: These can be secondary keywords or you can leave these as normal subheadings if it reads better for your end user.

Try to create a keyword rich title for your header tags where possible but always keep the focus on user readability. If it doesn't read right then don't keyword stuff your <h2> and <h3> tags.

<h4> tag: This tag is not necessary for your content and has no perceived SEO benefit. Many website owners reserve the <h4> tag for widget headers in the sidebar of their website.

<h5> tag: As for <h4> above. The <h5> tag, if used, is commonly found in the footer section of a website.

3. Keyword Density

Once upon a time, Google and the other search engines used to place a massive weight upon how many times your keyword appeared on the page and whether it was bolded, underlined and italicised.

Today, keyword density is almost redundant. Having gone through your website's page title and header tags, Google's algorithms are smart enough to figure out what your page is about by:

   i) What synonyms you use (related keywords)

   ii) The rest of your on page content (relevant material)

Attempts to keyword stuff may land you with an over optimisation penalty. Including your keyword once on the page, within the article content, is usually enough.

It is fine if your main keyword appears more than once on the page as long as it reads naturally in the context of your article.

If your content is over 500 words in length, you can repeat your main keyword (or preferably a synonym of it) but aim to keep the keyword density to 1% or below of your total content.

Note: the ranking weight given to Off Page SEO (i.e. anchor text backlinks and social shares) makes it possible for a website to appear in the SERPs for a keyword without that keyword even appearing in the content.

4. Keywords In The URL

Until 2013, having a keyword rich domain could help you to get an unfair advantage in the SERPs.

If you wanted to rank for 'dog training expert' for example, then buying an exact match domain (emd) like www.dogtrainingexpert.com (or whatever top level domain was appropriate for your country e.g. co.uk for the UK) would help you to rank faster for that keyword.

For many years, Black Hat marketers took advantage of emds to fill the SERPs with low quality spam sites, often with just a single page of content.

In an effort to reduce the amount of spam on show, Google has shifted priority in recent updates towards established brands and authority sites.

The reason is obvious: Google wants to provide quality results for its end users (to avoid them defecting to Yahoo and Bing) and authority sites provide a safe option.

In 2012, Google issued advice about removing the emd ranking advantage and by the end of 2013, the emd algorithm penalty kicked in.

The dilemma for Google in introducing the emd penalty was how to keep established brands at the top.

If someone is looking for a brand like Amazon, they expect to see www.amazon.com appear as the first result when they type 'Amazon' into the search box.

By contrast, a user looking for a dog training expert may not get the best solution if www.dogtrainingexpert.com appears as the first result in the SERPs. Businesses do not tend to brand themselves with the official company name 'Dog Training Expert'.

The Penguin 2.1 update, released on October 4, 2013, had a big impact on emd sites. The update was brought in to deal with over optimisation of anchor text and this affected a large number of emd sites. Big brands with authority survived the cull but smaller sites were hit.

A look at the SERPs today shows a much smaller number of emds ranking on the front page. Generally, the emds that rank now are sites that have age and authority.

If you own an emd that had authority and got hit by Penguin 2.1, it may be possible to bring your rankings back by dealing with any over optimisation. Speak to an SEO professional for help with this.

If your emd website had no authority (i.e. you were relying on the keyword rich url to give you a rankings boost), I recommend you now:

1. Create a 'slug' (also known as an inner page) with a keyword rich title, on a new, branded website. For example www.mydomain.com/dog-training-specialist

OR:

2. Create a keyword rich sub domain on a branded website and remove the 'www' canonicalization to help it look more natural.

To clarify point 2, you would use
http://dogtrainingspecialist.mydomain.com instead of
http://www.dogtrainingspecialist.mydomain.com

Both approaches are working right now. Creating a sub domain is more technical than creating a keyword rich inner page but is simple enough if you have a control panel for the backend of your website.

If you don't have control panel access then I recommend you contact your hosting company for support.

If you are trying to rank for a long tail keyword, i.e. more than two words, I recommend using the keyword rich inner page method. Having a long tail keyword rich subdomain can work but may look unnatural in the SERPs.

5. The Alternative

There is a third option which I haven't seen much discussion on. This is the partial match domain (pmd) option.

The pmd is where one or two of your keywords form part of the domain url. For example, www.dogtrainingcompany.com can be used to rank for 'dog training specialist'.

The pmd is a compromise that is working very well right now and I expect this trend to continue. There are thousands of sites that do not optimise for an emd but instead combine their brand name with a keyword, e.g. www.joesplumbingservice.com

If you go down this route, I recommend that you use an SEO professional. There is a fine balance between taking advantage of a pmd and losing the advantage with over optimisation.

6. The Sitemap

A sitemap is a file on your website that contains a list of all your website's URLs. The sitemap does not provide a direct ranking boost but can help you to get pages of your website, that haven't been crawled, indexed in the search engines.

Having more indexed pages gives you an opportunity to build more authority to your website.

If you rely on the search engines for traffic then your aim should be to get every page of your website indexed. Many websites have pages that don't get indexed because the search engines can't find these pages.

The search engines navigate their way across the web by following links. If some of your pages do not have any links (either internal or external links), there is a chance that these pages never got indexed. Installing a sitemap can help you to overcome this problem.

Some website owners choose not to index particular pages for a reason, e.g. if the content is protected or sensitive. Access to parts of your website can be controlled through the robots.txt file.

If you want more information about the robots.txt file visit: http://www.robotstxt.org/robotstxt.html

In WordPress it is simple to create a sitemap by using the Google XML sitemaps plugin.

To find out more about sitemaps visit http://www.sitemaps.org

7. Internal Links

An example of a website that makes good use of internal linking is wikipedia.org. You do not need to copy their linking structure but you should make sure that all the pages on your website are accessible to your visitors within a few clicks.

To achieve this you can create links from one page to another in an orderly fashion by using 'breadcrumbs'.

i. What Is A Breadcrumb?

A breadcrumb is a scheme to assist a user on a website with navigation. If you have lots of pages that are deep in your site and not linked to, it is possible that a visitor may not find these inner pages.

If it's difficult for a visitor to find these pages then it's likely that the search engines won't index those pages either.

Providing a breadcrumb trail can help your site to build authority by making it easier for the search engine spiders to crawl your website.

Ecommerce sites and other sites with a large amount of content can make good use of breadcrumbs to present their content in a hierarchical manner. eBay is an example of an ecommerce site that uses breadcrumbs effectively.

Breadcrumbs are usually arranged by:

page 1 > page 2 > page 3

If your site is single level then you don't need to use breadcrumbs. If you're unsure if breadcrumbs would improve your site navigation, construct a sitemap and take a look at all your pages.

Do certain pages fall into categories that could be logically navigated with the help of breadcrumbs?

The ideal place to use breadcrumbs is underneath the navigation header tabs, at the top of the web page. Use a small font to ensure that the breadcrumbs don't interfere with the content on the page.

ii. The Benefits Of Using Breadcrumbs

a. User convenience - provides easy navigation and enables the user to see exactly where they are and how they reached that page.

b. Reduce clicks - user no longer needs to keep clicking the back button in their browser to return to previous pages.

c. Can reduce bounce rates - if a user sees related pages it can make them curious to see what else of interest is on the website.

d. Improve crawl rate - easy navigation means that the search engine spiders are more likely to reach deep inner pages and index them too, which in turn helps to build the site's authority.

If you have a large website with a complex structure then you may want to hire a website designer to help you code a script that will enable breadcrumbs.

If your website is small you can create breadcrumbs manually:

a. List the navigation path to each page that will have breadcrumbs. Start with the home page and move through the website to determine the path from the home page to every inner page. Make a note of these path lists.

b. Write the HTML code for the navigation path. You can use free tools like the html editor, CoffeeCup, or a text editor like Notepad. Create a hyperlink for each page in the breadcrumb trail with the HTML <a> tag.

   For user convenience, place a separator between the pages in the breadcrumb trail. Commonly used separators include > or - . The HTML code should give you a sequence that looks like:

   <a href="http://www.site.com/">Home</a> > <a href="http://www.site.com/page1">Page 1</a> > <a href="http://www.site.com/page2">Page 2</a> > <a href="http://www.site.com/page3">Page 3</a> and so on.

   On the web page the breadcrumb trail would display as:

   Home > Page 1 > Page 2 > Page 3

c. Insert the code that is relevant for each particular page. The best place for the code is at the top of the page just below the header. Reduce the font size of the breadcrumb links to avoid obscuring the content.

d. Many websites use navigation tabs in the top menu and in these cases there is no need to display a breadcrumb on the home page.

Based on the sample code in part b, a site structure that goes deeper than three pages would need to add additional HTML code for each additional page.

e. After you have created the breadcrumbs for each page, go back and test the code to check that each hyperlink takes you to the previous page and also to the next page in that breadcrumb trail.

Any broken links will affect your user navigation and also how the search engines crawl through your site.

For more information about using breadcrumbs visit Google's support section:

https://support.google.com/webmasters/answer/185417?hl =en

iii. Ecommerce Site Example

eBay's home page displays the following navigation tabs:

Let's click on the middle navigation tab 'Electronics'.

Immediately, we are presented with a navigation menu on the left hand side and the website shows you in 'breadcrumbs' where you are on the site.

You can keep clicking on the navigation tabs until you are presented with a list of products to purchase.

The navigation experience takes us from the home page to the electronics section and then to a sub section as follows:

The breadcrumbs trail is:

Home > Electronics > Cameras & Photography

The trail allows a user to navigate back to the Electronics section by clicking on the blue 'Electronics' link and even to go back to the homepage by clicking on the blue 'Home' link.

The two hyperlinks in blue are internal anchor text links.

iv. Internal Link Juice Flow

The home page of a website carries the most authority. When a site has good internal link structure, authority or 'link juice' can flow from the home page to the inner pages.

This is how a website with authority, e.g. Wikipedia, has inner pages that rank high in the search engines for multiple keywords.

Creating breadcrumb trails on a large website is a much better method of directing the flow of link juice than going down the manual route of internal linking.

Internal linking can provide a strong boost to On Page SEO if it is done correctly. I recommend that you use an SEO professional to help structure your internal linking and turn your website into an authority in your niche.

8. External Links

An external link is a link from your website to a different site.

i. Relevant Authority Links

Today, we have found that relevant external links on your website can actually give your site a moderate rankings boost in Google's algorithm.

Previously, I have referenced the need to keep the flow of link juice within a website by using internal links. The concept of providing a relevant link, i.e. to another site in your niche may sound foreign.

Why would you want to do this?

It is because Google looks at the Internet from a holistic view. Linking from your website to another relevant website that has authority has two effects:

a. It improves user experience by providing a visitor with the opportunity to find out more information on what they are searching for.

b. It associates your site with an authority site which helps to build trust with Google.

By helping user experience and Google to crawl the web more easily, you earn a few "brownie points".

Genuine authority websites focus less on SEO and more on how they can benefit user experience. It makes sense for a website in the medical niche to link to another website that is in the same niche or a related niche, e.g. dentistry or optometry.

A website that does not link out may raise some flags. White Hat SEO involves building relationships with other website owners and acquiring links naturally.

If you are integrating into the wider Internet community and picking up natural inbound links then it also makes sense for you to externally link to other sites that will enhance your reputation.

ii. Bad Neighbourhoods Checklist

Be careful that you do not link out to 'bad neighbourhoods'.

Google does not provide a clear definition of what a bad neighbourhood is so I have included the following checklist based on personal experience and from our peers:

a. Any site that is spammy in nature - e.g. adult, gambling and pharmaceutical websites that claim to sell 'magic pills' online.

b. Sites that scrape content from other blogs. Not to be confused with sites that provide quality curation, i.e. provide a link back to the original source and enhance the content with their own spin, e.g. The Huffington Post.

c. Sites that have a large amount of duplicate content.

d. Sites with a large amount of outbound links -> commonly referred to as 'link farms'.

e. Blogs with hundreds of unmoderated comments.

9. Broken Links

As a site gets older it is common for broken links to appear. The further a post or page disappears into the depths of a website, the less attention it receives and the less likely it is for a broken link to be fixed.

An internal link can get broken when a change is made to a page (e.g. an update causing the url of that page to change). More common though is the external broken link. This can occur when an owner of a domain chooses not to renew the registration or the hosting.

Broken links on your site can bleed Page Rank. To find out if you have a broken link you can install a browser plugin called 'Check My Links' in the Chrome browser.

The plugin works by crawling through your website and highlighting which links work and which ones are broken. You can also check for broken links on other websites.

You can use this tool to help build a new relationship with another site owner.

If you are willing to get creative, you can create content that is similar to where the broken link points to and then ask the site owner to point the link to a page on your website for an extra backlink.

Use The Wayback Machine at http://archive.org/web to find out what the original content was about and write something similar.

This method can be a powerful way of picking up a link from a website that has age and authority. This strategy works best for websites that are relevant to your niche.

10. Use Of Media

In the early days of the Internet, websites were text based because of slow dial up speed restrictions. This changed with the introduction of broadband and 3G mobile which made access to the Internet much faster.

Modern technology evolves and access to the Internet is getting faster with access to fibre optic and 4G mobile now widely available for many users.

This means that your website can provide a much richer experience through images and video. There are many benefits to using media on your website. It helps your website to stand out and creates a better experience for users.

Images catch our attention and also help to break up content, making it easier to read. Videos can help you to engage with your users. The longer a user stays on your website the better chance you have of converting them.

Like the content? Help us by sharing it!

A user that enjoys your content is likely to share it with others. You can help your content to be shared by including social share buttons next to your articles, e.g. to Facebook, Twitter and other social media platforms.

Social share buttons can help bring additional traffic and also give your website a rankings boost through social sharing. In WordPress it is easy to install a social sharing plugin.

The time spent on a website and visitor bounce rate are becoming more important as a ranking factor. How much importance they hold is relative to other sites in your niche.

Remember that Google is a bot and it therefore relies on metrics like how long a user stays on a website and whether they click through to other pages on a website as indicators of how relevant that site is to the keyword phrase that the user put into the search box.

More information on bounce rate is provided on Google's support page:

https://support.google.com/analytics/answer/1009409?hl=en-GB

A website with a high bounce rate, i.e. only a few users click through to another page on the website, is an indication to the search engines that your site isn't relevant for what users are searching for.

By contrast, a site with less authority or fewer backlinks may end up higher than yours if visitors are spending more time on it.

Having good quality content, combined with effective use of media, can help a visitor to spend more time on your website.

Bounce rate can be tracked through tools like Google Analytics.

For best practice, keep the file size of any images on your web pages small. For video, use a hosting platform like YouTube or Vimeo and paste the embed code into your web page instead of self hosting.

11. Site Speed

How fast your site loads plays a big factor in whether a user even gets to read your content. If your site takes more than 10 seconds to load you should look at ways of 'trimming the fat' or you may risk losing a chunk of your visitors.

Today, Google estimates that almost half of all queries in its search engine now come from a mobile device. With 3G and 4G coverage still patchy in some areas it makes sense to have a website that loads fast and is mobile friendly.

This means reducing heavy loading images (your website developer or SEO professional can help you to optimise your existing images), getting rid of scripts that take time to load (e.g. Java), or moving to a faster, dedicated server.

It is good practice to test your website load time from a different browser or someone else's computer. This is because your regular browser will cache your website in memory and this can distort your load time because your results are skewed.

The faster your website loads the better your end user experience will be. The search engines like a website that provides good user experience and will reward them with a rankings boost. A fast loading website also makes it easier for the search engine spiders to crawl your website.

Google has a tool that shows you how long it takes for your site to load and what steps you can take to help speed up the load time:

http://developers.google.com/speed/pagespeed/insights

The tool can also be used on your inner pages as well as the home page.

If your site runs on WordPress there are plugins that can help you to speed up your website like WP Super Cache or W3 Total Cache. These plugins work by generating static html pages instead of php files.

I recommend that you only use one type of plugin to optimise the load time of your website. Installing two plugins that claim to do the same job can result in conflicts.

In WordPress, it can be tempting to install every available plugin that you can find a use for. Keep in mind that each plugin has its own footprint. The more plugins you have, the 'heavier' your site becomes.

Each plugin provides its own function and a browser will not usually display a site to the end user until all functions on that web page are complete.

12. Mobile Friendly

Access to the Internet from a mobile device continues to grow at a rapid pace as smartphones and tablets become globally prevalent. In less developed countries, e.g. some nations in Africa, mobile is the main source for users to access the Internet.

If your site is not mobile friendly (e.g. you use Flash technology) then you'll be alienating a large chunk of your online traffic. A user that cannot access your content will navigate away to a competitor's site.

Having a mobile friendly site can help to improve your bounce rate and also how long a user spends on your website and so will indirectly contribute towards to your site's ranking.

If your website shows up in the local business listings, e.g. Google Places, it is even more important that your site is mobile friendly.

A large number of users that search for a local business use a mobile device and you can boost your conversion rate by having features like 'tap to call' and 'maps'.

Tap to call takes advantage of a phone's calling function to put the user directly through to the business. This means they don't have to fiddle around with a pen and paper trying to manually write your business number down.

Maps takes advantage of a mobile's GPS function to show the user how far they are from the business and can provide them with directions.

There are two ways to make a website mobile friendly:

a. Use a responsive theme that resizes the content on a website according to the screen size of the device that is accessing the website.

b. Use a mobile website that your visitor is redirected to when they land on your main website from a mobile device.

13. On Page Optimisation Check List

1. Put your main keyword in the website title.

2. Add the header tags <h1>, <h2> and <h3>.

3. Create relevant content for your readers. Base the content on the keyword that you want to rank for. Write content for your users, not the search engines, i.e. do not keyword stuff. Try to include the keyword near the beginning of your content, for example in one of the header tags.

4. Use media (images and video) to help break up the content and keep the user engaged. Optimise the file size of images and use an external hosting site for videos e.g. YouTube or Vimeo.

5. Rename some of your images with your keyword before you include them in your article, e.g. dogtrainingspecialist.jpg.

   The search engines cannot see images. Instead, they determine what an image is about by looking at the details in the meta description of that image (file properties) or by comparing it to other stock photos across the web.

6. Add alt tags that include your keyword to one or two images on the page. Do not over optimise every single image with an alt tag keyword.

7. If you are using video in the page then make sure the title of the video is related to the content of your page.

8. Use a sitemap and internal links to help your website pages get crawled and indexed by the search engines. Consider use of breadcrumbs if your site is large.

9. Check for broken links, particularly on inner pages that may get less attention, e.g. older blog posts. This can be done in the Chrome browser by using the 'Check My Links' plugin.

10. Link out to an authority site from within your content to help build trust with the search engines and improve user experience.

    Make sure that you avoid linking out to 'bad neighbourhoods' e.g. spammy sites with poor quality content or sites that are in the porn, gambling and pharmaceuticals industry.

11. Find out how fast your site loads. A slow loading site will put off your visitors before they even have a chance to access your content.

12. Consider using a responsive theme or mobile website to make your website mobile friendly. This is even more important if your website is in the local listings like Google Places, where a large number of visitors will be searching for your products or services from their mobile device.

Chapter 5 Summary

Key Takeaways

In Chapter 5 you learnt the following:

1. The importance of your website title for good On Page SEO.

2. How to optimise the header tags with your keywords.

3. Taking advantage of a keyword rich domain without incurring a penalty.

4. The correct way to structure your site with internal links for maximum link juice flow and user accessibility.

5. How to check for a broken link to avoid bleeding Page Rank.

6. Using media to enrich the user experience and getting your content shared through social media buttons.

7. How to optimise your site speed for mobile traffic.

What To Expect In Chapter 6

In the next chapter we'll cover powerful marketing strategies to help you build relationships with industry leaders and position you as an authority.

We'll also learn how to capture a larger audience by taking your existing content and repurposing it into different formats. Repurposing has additional benefits: you'll naturally acquire quality backlinks to boost your online profile.

Chapter 6

White Hat SEO

Why perform White Hat SEO? The main reason is for long term sustainability.

Google's algorithms have become increasingly sophisticated and common Black Hat SEO tactics that used to work, e.g. keyword stuffing by matching the colour of text to the web page background or spamming your website with thousands of links in a short space of time, will now land you with a penalty.

If you discover a Black Hat SEO loophole that still works, keep in mind that your rankings are likely to be short lived.

If you want to stop living in fear of the next algorithm update then you need to adopt an attitude of building your business for the long term.

This means using the White Hat SEO tactics that Google encourages (more information is available on its YouTube channel) to boost your rankings naturally and build your brand in the process.

1. Interview Experts

One of the best ways to get new visitors to your content and pick up useful authority backlinks in the process is by interviewing experts in your niche. A key to online success is to work with your competition not against them.

If you want to fast track your results online then it makes sense to get your content in front of your target audience, i.e. people who are looking for your content and who will appreciate it.

With millions of blogs online there is a good chance that you already have competitors in your niche. If you can find a blog with traffic that is complementary to yours, you can contact that owner and leverage their existing traffic by interviewing them.

As long as your blog isn't a direct copy of theirs, you should have a good chance of securing an interview. Look for blogs in your niche that provide related information but from a different angle.

This could mean researching for blogs that go deeper on a particular topic. Or you could try looking for blog owners that have different content to your own, but whose material feels like a natural extension to your existing content.

Experts like to get interviewed because it makes them feel important. You should tailor the questions that you ask the expert to fit in with what your readers would find useful.

Here are a few sample questions that you can ask in the interview:

I.   How did you get started?

II. What are the 3 biggest mistakes you made en route to your success?

III. Who were your mentors and what did you learn from them?

IV.   If someone was starting new, what tips would you give them to help them be successful?

V.   How does your product/service help others?

VI.   How long does it take to achieve success with your methods?

VII. What's the best way for people to contact you?

Skype is a free platform that you can use to interview an expert. You can record the interview in mp3 format with a plugin like Pamela or Call Recorder. After the interview is complete, post it onto your website and let the blog owner know.

Experts love to have their ego massaged so there is a good chance that they will link to the interview from their own website and let any users on their email newsletter list know too.

You can help get the word out about the interview by posting to your own social media platforms and asking them to do the same.

Even a few shares on social media can help to give your site a boost. Google will notice these social shares and the additional traffic coming in and reward your site in the SERPs.

If you are new to your niche then you should be realistic with the response rate that you get when asking to interview experts. Before people give you their time they want to know what's in it for them.

In the beginning, you may need to prove that you have an audience of subscribers to your blog or followers on social media. Getting started on social media is free and you can easily build up a following by posting content from your blog onto social media platforms.

On Twitter, you can follow users in your niche and a percentage of them will follow you back. When you create short messages on Twitter (called tweets), your followers will see your information and engage with you. By posting information of value you can quickly build up an audience of followers.

On LinkedIn, you can join groups and participate in the conversations by posting information of value and also by answering the questions that are getting posted by other users.

The same principles apply in other social media platforms like Facebook and Google Plus. Engage with other users and post information that is of value to them.

Once you have built up a following, it will be easier to get interviews with experts in your niche. You can also find experts that are active on social media and ask to interview them too.

With persistence it is possible to build your brand by connecting with other blog owners and experts on social media. If you consistently repeat this strategy of interviewing experts you can quickly position yourself as an authority in your niche.

Once you have the interviews, you should make them available in different formats on your website as people like to consume content in different ways.

An mp3 can be easily transcribed and turned into a pdf for users to download. You can also create a video by using PowerPoint slides. Take the important content from the interview and summarise it into bullet points in these slides.

Adding images of you and the expert onto the slides is a powerful way of getting users to associate you with that expert.

Use screen capture software, e.g. Camstudio to record the slideshow. The mp3 of the interview forms the audio part whilst the slides become the visual part of the video.

To help drive additional traffic you can upload your slides to SlideShare and upload the video to YouTube. Another benefit of uploading content to both SlideShare and YouTube is the opportunity to get authority backlinks to your own website.

2. Build Authority, Become A Leader

i. Curate Content

Sites that curate content from a variety of sources, like news feed aggregators, can position themselves as a 'go to' site.

Curation is the process of scraping content from another website and then adding unique fresh content, i.e. the curation website owner adds their own spin.

It is important to give a link back to the original site to avoid duplicate content penalties in Google.

Curation can be as simple as scraping 250 words from a 700 word article and then adding 150 words of fresh content with a link back to the original source.

Readers of the site that is curating content can benefit in two ways. First, they can view the source link and read the original content. Second, they can read the curating website owner's opinion and then see if they agree with it.

The Huffington Post is a website that curates content from multiple websites across the web and drives huge traffic back to the site.

In 2011, AOL bought the Huffington Post for a huge $315m. The site was only 6 years old, having launched in 2005.

People like to visit one site that pools relevant industry news from a variety of sources as it saves them the effort of manually going to each site individually. Curating content can be a great way to drive natural backlinks to your site.

ii. Create Industry Awards

Creating an award within your industry requires leadership and consistent effort but the rewards can be huge. There is a lot of 'noise' in the online space, with hundreds of businesses vying for our attention, and this can make it difficult for a startup to get noticed and start building authority.

Getting a badge of recognition is a great way for a business to stand out from the competition and build authority.

Recognising businesses or experts can be as simple as creating a logo for that business, with your brand details on it, and setting up a page on your website that shows the list of 'winners'.

This method does require consistent action if you want to gain credibility and be taken seriously by your peers. Be prepared to invest resources into networking with businesses in your industry.

You could start with a monthly leaderboard that you post on your website of the top 50 'movers and shakers' in your industry. In time you can progress to an offline event like a dinner/dance where you hand out awards that recognise the contributions of that business or expert to your industry.

You can test this method for free using social media platforms like Facebook and Twitter. Reach out to new entrants in your industry as these will be the ones most eager to build their profiles.

Once you have a sufficient number of interested parties, you can use this audience as 'social proof' and post onto social media platforms like LinkedIn, which is taken more seriously as a business networking site.

Create a group on LinkedIn and invite members to join by contacting all the businesses in your industry.

When established and successful business owners see that your group is rapidly growing they will be more inclined to join too.

iii. Social Media Badges

Building up your social media profiles with followers who share your content is an excellent way to create authority. People like to follow experts, celebrities and businesses that are successful.

Once you have a respectable amount of followers you can market this by adding social media badges on your website. Badges make it easy for visitors that land on your website to connect with you.

Google Plus is rapidly growing as a social media platform and is also having a major role in Google's ranking algorithm. To create a Google Plus badge, login to your Google account with your gmail address and head over to https://developers.google.com/+/web/badge.

If you're logged in then you'll be presented with a page like this:

On the page you are presented with options to edit the code. For example you can change the badge so that it displays in landscape format instead of the default portrait and you can also make the badge light or dark.

If you are converting to landscape then you need to select a minimum width of 273 pixels.

You can update your profile picture within your Google Plus account if you want to change your 'headshot' or you can use a logo image instead of your picture.

Once you're happy with the changes copy the entire code into your website. A popular place to display your badge is in a widget in the sidebar. The Google Plus badge will display how many followers you have.

A social media badge provides several benefits:

a. Build trust - readers will see your profile picture and identify with you. This immediately sets you apart from other 'lifeless' blogs.

b. The badge acts as a social signal both for your readers and for Google.

c. Having a respectable amount of followers will position you as an authority in your niche.

3. Write Epic Content For Natural Links

In the offline space, i.e. a brick and mortar business, the biggest factor in attracting new traffic is the geographic location.

A business that is located in a busy high street or shopping mall doesn't need to rely heavily on finding new ways to market themselves. In this situation the adage 'build it and they will come' holds true.

Unfortunately, it doesn't work like this in the online space. A new business has to make an effort to attract visitors to their website and it's not enough to have a great looking design.

– Traffic is the lifeblood of any online business –

There are numerous ways to get traffic, including paid advertising in the search engines or on social media platforms like Facebook. The problem with paid traffic is that it's like a tap. Switch off the paid ads and the traffic stops flowing.

Free traffic sources, like building an audience on social media, require an investment of your time. If you are dedicated to running your own business then it can be hard to be consistent in your social media efforts.

Google advocates that you write great content in order to drive traffic back to your website.

The problem for startups is that there are millions of blogs online so even if you get a few people to read your content, e.g. on social media, it could take you months or years before you get enough traffic to make your business sustainable.

In the online space hope is not a strategy. You can build a website but unfortunately without good marketing 'they will not come'.

If you're on a budget and don't have the resources to pay for your traffic then you need to get creative while you wait for your website to rank in the organic listings of the SERPs.

A strategy that you can start with today is to find authority blogs within your niche that already receive a healthy volume of traffic. Go deep into the blogs and look for older posts from 2 or 3 years ago.

Not all of the information in a blog is 'evergreen content'.

Here is where you can find opportunities to write updates to older, popular blog posts. Find a new twist on an older blog post or re-write that blog post with fresh up to date information.

Then contact the blog owner and offer it to them as a guest post. If you give the blog owner due credit and reference them in your post, there is a good chance that they will accept your offer.

If the blog owner refuses to let you guest post on their site you can always go back and ask for a link from their website. The key here is that you're adding value to their readers and this is what you need to emphasise to them.

If your content is useful to their audience they may even send an email to their subscriber list and this can be a great way to leverage their existing traffic.

If this strategy doesn't work with the first blog owner that you contact don't give up. There are plenty of blog owners that are desperate for quality content so persist with your efforts.

You can still find ways to leverage some of their traffic by posting the article to your own website and then promoting the post on the blog owner's social media profiles and your own.

The content is relevant to that blog owner's audience so they will be interested in what you write.

If your content is epic, i.e. the reader identifies with it or finds incredible value then you stand a good chance of picking up natural shares.

This will give you a better chance to convert some of that blog owner's traffic into your own.

To help you get more shares you need to be proactive and ask your readers to take action.

Under each post include a message like:

"If you enjoyed this content please share it on your Facebook page or by hitting one of the other social buttons below".

Having an audience will make it easier to build relationships with other leaders in your industry and to position yourself as an authority.

Blog owners are constantly looking for ways to increase their exposure and sharing other people's content on Twitter, Facebook, Google Plus and other social media platforms can help to create tremendous good will.

Smart blog owners use metrics like Google Analytics to track the number of visitors to their website.

If they see a surge in traffic based on your efforts then you can be sure that some of them will look to reciprocate the favour.

The more exposure you create for others, the more you are likely to receive in return. By adding value to your audience you will naturally attract more interest in your products and services.

Fostering strong relationships with other leaders in your industry will make it easier for you to promote your post the next time that you create some epic content.

The obvious benefits include more traffic, more links and more subscribers to your website. The bigger picture is that you'll be positioning yourself as a leader and authority in your niche.

4. Fresh Content And Conversions

In late 2011, Google introduced a freshness factor into its algorithms to help display relevant results to its end users. When you write content for your website you should aim to make it 'evergreen'.

This means being relevant for a long period of time, as opposed to covering a current event which no one will be interested in after a few days or weeks.

Unless you are in a news related niche, the content on your home page should be relevant for users whether they land on your site today or in a few months time.

If you are selling a product or providing a service then your home page should focus on the features and benefits. Include some valuable take aways for people that are not ready to buy. This will help to build trust and rapport.

The home page is a good place to let your visitors know how you differentiate yourself from the competition.

If a user lands on a site that has similar content to every other site then they'll typically go with a site that looks trustworthy (usually based on how good the site looks) or whoever is offering the lowest price.

When you are building a new website it is easy to stay fresh for the search engines because you are constantly adding new pages or posts and updating the website to get it looking how you want.

When the site is completed it can be difficult to maintain the 'freshness' because your main work is done. This is where maintaining a blog can help to keep your site fresh.

The more indexed pages a website has the greater the chance of acquiring more backlinks and social shares to both the inner pages and to the home page.

Authority starts to build when a site picks up more links and shares. A site that doesn't add new content on a regular basis, whether it's daily or weekly, is not providing its readers with a reason to come back.

A website is like virtual real estate and needs maintenance. Readers know when a website is neglected. If you allow your site to fall flat then your traffic will also fall. A site with no traffic will struggle to stay in business.

Many business owners are confused about how often they should be updating their blog. This comes down to personal preference but you should be influenced by how often your competition updates their site.

This doesn't mean that you need to behave like a news channel and add content every single day, unless you wish to, but you should be aiming to update your site at least once a week.

In recent algorithm updates Google has been giving preference in the SERPs to established brands and authority sites. This shift has occurred because Google wants to serve up quality content to its end users.

The days of having a thin site (e.g. a single page or just a few pages) and ranking it high in the SERPs are gone. You may get away with a thin site in a low competition niche but if you want to protect your rankings for the long term then you need to build authority and this stems from regular content.

Getting ideas for new content can be a challenge. One solution is to look at the industry news and put your own spin on the new updates that come out.

If something is trending then you should jump on it as this is a great opportunity for you to attract new readers to your website.

You may need to be a little creative if the trend is not directly related to your niche but there's no reason why you can't leverage a major event and create new content.

For example, if your website is in the law niche and you want to jump on the new Apple iPhone launch, you could write something about the ongoing legal dispute between Apple and Samsung in regards to their patents.

Explain how the new product may affect the relationship between these technology giants.

If your website is about business then you could focus on both Apple's and Samsung's marketing efforts and how effective it's been relative to the number of phones that each company has sold.

Readers expect authority sites to be amongst the first to cover breaking news. You can receive the latest updates in your industry by subscribing to news feed aggregators like Google Alerts and then creating useful content.

Having visitors return to your website on a regular basis helps to build trust and makes it more likely that they will purchase from you instead of your competitors.

This is why maintaining a blog and being consistent in your efforts to share content across different social media platforms is so powerful.

Google recognises this as White Hat SEO. Building strong relationships will help your content to get shared, allow you to acquire natural backlinks and provide you with long term sustainability for your business.

5. Finding Relevant Blogs In Your Niche

To help you get started with the White Hat strategies above you need to connect with other blog owners in your niche. Use the search string in Google to find blogs in your niche and leave an intelligent comment that adds value to the post.

This will help you to pick up a relevant backlink and drive traffic back to your website. Adding value to the blog post will also help to get the attention of the blog owner.

If we are looking for dog training blogs then we would enter the following search string into Google:

dog training inurl:blog intitle:submit post

This returns the following result:

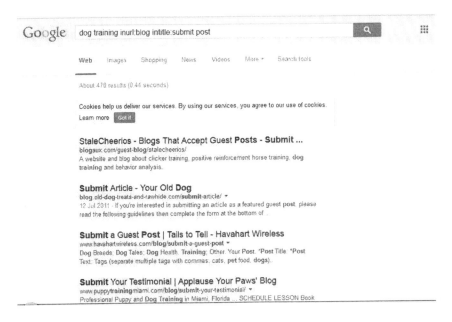

Google returns about 478 results. If these results are too narrow you can try a broader search by just using a single keyword e.g. 'dog'.

So we would use:

dog inurl:blog intitle:submit post

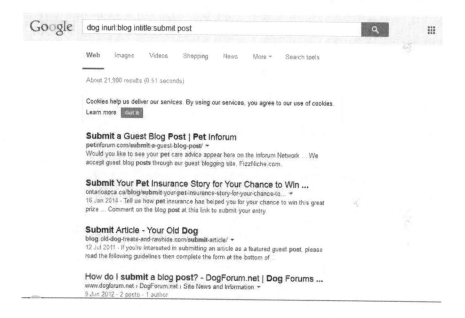

By shortening the keyword, we now have a huge 21,900 results.

To get results relevant for your niche you can replace the words 'dog training' or 'dog' with your own keywords in the search string.

6. Get A Business Listing

If you own a brick and mortar business then you can pick up a backlink by submitting your website to a directory. To submit an online business to a directory you need to have an address.

This can be either your home address or you can use a virtual office. Adding a telephone line will help you look professional. Use a landline for credibility. Established businesses use landlines not mobiles.

Tip: To get a virtual office run a search in your preferred search engine for virtual office <your city>.

It's worth noting that most directories are garbage. Unless they have existing authority it's not worth submitting a link to them. There are a few that are worth using though and these are listed below.

Some of these directories may incur a recurring cost.

dir.yahoo.com (PR8)

www.dmoz.org (PR7)

botw.org (PR7)

www.yell.com/free-listing (PR7)

www.manta.com (PR6)

Note: The Yellow Pages has rebranded to Hibu so you may see references to their new name if you create a listing with them.

7. Repurposing Your Content

In today's society, people consume content in different ways. Some like to download video and watch it on their tablet device whilst others prefer listening to audio through an mp3 player or their smartphone.

If you are only providing written content on your blog then you could be putting off a large part of your audience who don't have the time or opportunity to be near a device that is connected to the Internet.

Consider commuters on the train or bus or those who drive their car on the way into work.

If you want to grow your target audience then you need to cater for all the mediums through which your audience can connect with you and consume your content.

The easiest way is to create a blog and just put all your thoughts down into a written article. The problem with blogs is that there are millions of blogs on the Internet now. This makes it much harder to stand out from your competitors.

Repurposing your content into different formats can help you to pick up more traffic and get more backlinks to your site.

If your content is good then it will also get shared. You can repurpose your content into the different formats listed below:

i. Create A Presentation

Take your article and create multiple slides in PowerPoint (or Keynote if you're on a Mac).

Upload the presentation to slideshare.net which is a PR8 site.

Other presentation websites that you may wish to consider uploading to include:

www.scribd.com (PR8)

www.authorstream.com (PR6)

www.slideboom.com (PR5)

ii. Create A PDF

Convert your Microsoft Word .doc file into a .pdf and upload it to popular pdf sharing sites like:

www.docstoc.com (PR7)

www.calameo.com (PR7).

Tip: If you are running Microsoft Office 2007 and do not have the 'Save As' PDF feature then you can download the Microsoft add in from:

http://www.microsoft.com/en-us/download/confirmation.aspx?id=9943

- note, if the above link has changed then go to Microsoft.com and navigate to the download center. In the search box enter 'save as pdf'.

iii. Create A Video

There are numerous ways to create a video. Windows offers a free tool, Windows Movie Maker and on an Apple Mac, there is iMovie.

If you have already repurposed your blog article into a presentation you can create a video slideshow using screen recording software. On a PC you can use tools like CamStudio (free) or Camtasia (paid).

If you are on a Mac there is QuickTime (free) or ScreenFlow (paid) and Camtasia (paid). You can add audio by recording your voice with a microphone or by adding background music.

Using paid software will make it easier for your video to look professional.

The obvious platform to upload a video to is YouTube but there are also other video sharing sites that get a lot of traffic and that rank well in the search engines.

Consider:

vimeo.com (PR9)

www.dailymotion.com (PR8)

www.metacafe.com (PR6)

iv. Create A Podcast

If you have already created a video and recorded a voiceover for your slides, you can strip the audio from the video with free software.

In Windows Movie Maker you can drag the video to the audio timeline and then publish the movie into a .wma audio file.

If you prefer to create an .mp3 audio file then download the free version of AoA Audio Extractor. On a Mac you can use iTunes to strip the audio from a video.

If you want to record or edit an .mp3 you can use the free software Audacity. After installing the software you'll need to install the lame mp3 plugin.

Audacity is an excellent tool that works on both Windows and Mac.

Once you have your audio file, upload it to podcast directories like:

www.blubrry.com (PR5)

www.allpodcasts.com (PR5)

www.mirpod.com/addpodcast.php?lang=en (PR4).

v. Create An Infographic

Infographics are in vogue right now and chances are that you've seen them posted on Facebook, Pinterest and other social media platforms.

For SEO professionals, infographics are a great way to pick up a relatively untapped source of backlinks.

An infographic is a way of putting complex information into a visual format, i.e. an image with text.

Infographics are eye catching and easy to understand and can be a great way to pick up an authority backlink from a site that may not otherwise link back to yours.

If you have experience with graphic design, e.g. Adobe Photoshop, you can create your own infographics. You can also hire a professional designer to create one for you.

If you're on a budget then you need to get creative. You can make basic designs in Microsoft PowerPoint but if you haven't got PowerPoint then download free office suite alternatives like KingSoft or Libre Office.

In PowerPoint, choose a background slide, write your text and take a screenshot with the Print Screen button on your keyboard.

Save the screenshot as an image in Microsoft Paint and you now have an infographic.

If you're willing to roll your sleeves up and create a professional looking infographic you can head over to sites like Infogr.am, Piktochart.com or Venngage.com.

YouTube has tutorial videos to help you create a professional looking infographic on these sites.

Once you're happy with your infographic, upload it to the following sites to get a backlink:

www.pinterest.com (PR9)

dailyinfographic.com (PR6)

www.coolinfographics.com (PR6)

Don't forget you can also post your infographic to other social media profiles.

An infographic that has useful content can be a powerful way to market your brand.

On social media sites you also have an opportunity to pick up social shares, acquire natural backlinks and help drive traffic back to your website.

Chapter 6 Summary

Key Takeaways

In Chapter 6 you learnt the following:

1. The importance of leveraging authority by interviewing experts in your industry.

2. How to position yourself as a leader by making your website the go to place in your industry.

3. Why creating regular quality content will help to build your authority.

4. Search strings to enter into Google to help you find relevant blogs in your niche.

5. Top websites to get an authority business listing from.

6. How to repurpose your content to syndicate it across different platforms and build your audience.

What To Expect In Chapter 7

In the next chapter we'll cover how to avoid an over optimisation penalty from Penguin.

We'll learn the difference between different link types and how to build trust with Google by creating a natural backlink profile. This will help to protect your site from future algorithm updates.

Chapter 7

Advanced Off Page SEO - Link Building Like A Pro

1. Natural Link Building

In the past few years, Google and the other major search engines have changed their algorithms to give priority to natural link building. If a site is new then it's not realistic for it to receive hundreds or thousands of links every day.

A site that accumulates a large amount of backlinks in a short space of time will raise flags unless you have accumulated trust with the search engines.

Building trust for a new domain requires patience. You should produce original content on a regular basis and make efforts to market this content through different channels.

If you attempt to shortcut the link building process to a new domain then it's likely that you'll find yourself in a sandbox.

This means that your site may disappear from the search results or be pushed back several pages for a period of time.

Natural link building is about encompassing White Hat strategies.

If you are starting out then I recommend you build your social media profiles. Links (social shares) from social media platforms are interpreted by the search engines as natural links.

Google's algorithm for social links is still in its infancy right now so having a large amount of social media links will not bring you a penalty.

If you understand how media is shared across different social media platforms then it should be obvious why. If a post, image or video becomes popular then it can quickly go viral.

This will means hundreds, if not thousands of shares, within a short space of time.

For now, social media shares are the safest links that you can get without needing to worrying about penalties.

However, our tests have shown that a rankings boost from social media links only provides a short term boost.

If you put this into perspective then it makes sense. People are not interested in what happened a few weeks ago.

- Today's news is tomorrow's garbage paper -

2. Link Velocity

Whether your website is a few days old or several years old, it looks odd to the search engines if a site picks up a large amount of links in a short space of time.

If you are engaging in an SEO campaign for the first time then you should start your link building very slowly and build up over time.

To begin with, create content on a consistent basis, e.g. daily or several times a week and share this content across different social media sites.

If you have a decent following on your social media profiles and your content is good then it will get picked up and earn you some natural backlinks.

As your site starts to mature you can start feeding in new links but aim for consistency. It does not look natural if your site picks up 300 links in a month and then none for the next month.

There is no fixed number of links that you can build to your site within a short period of time before you incur a penalty but if you start slow and gradually increase the link velocity then you should avoid any flags.

Before you start your SEO campaigns it is important to research how many backlinks your competitors have and how old their domains are.

If you are operating in a local market then you may only need a few hundred back links to get onto the front page of the SERPs.

As the search engine algorithms become more sophisticated it is important to mimic natural link building behaviour.

If a piece of content is becoming popular then it will get shared across different platforms and this will result in backlinks and additional traffic to the originator's website.

The traffic that comes into a website can be tracked through Google Analytics.

If your analytics show a low number of visitors but the number of inbound links stays high, this is clearly disproportionate to how natural links are built and could raise a flag against your site, especially if it is new.

When a piece of content goes truly viral, the originator's site experiences a sharp spike in traffic and links come in from a wide variety of platforms like article directories, forum posts, social bookmarking sites, web 2.0 sites and wiki sites, as well as social media.

The more natural your link building strategy, the more successful your SEO campaign will be.

If your site has some age then you can get away with a higher link velocity but if you want to play safe then I recommend starting with a handful of links and slowly ramping it up after a few weeks.

The key to link building velocity is consistency. If your content is getting shared then it doesn't look natural to have 300 links built one month and nothing the next month.

If however you are building 7 links per day for the first two weeks and then you bump this up to 10 links per day for the next few weeks, this looks far more natural and will save you from a penalty.

3. Not All Links Are Equal

It is estimated that over half of the web pages on the Internet are spam.

In an effort to remove these results from show, the search engines have allocated a measure of trust to different types of links.

A link from an authority website with age and trust will carry far more weight than a link from a website that is only a few months old.

Having a few high quality links will give you more of a rankings boost than thousands of low quality links.

If you focus on producing good content then you will have a better chance of acquiring high quality links over time.

It's worth noting that in a natural link profile a website will pick up a range of different link types.

So even if your site does pick up a few undesirable links then you will still be fine as long as your link profile has a balance of low and high quality links.

Quality Checklist:

i. Lowest quality - links from a bad neighbourhood, e.g. pills, porn and gambling, comment spam and link farms.

ii. Low quality - forum signatures, reciprocal links, poor quality directories, footer links.

iii. Medium quality - social media profiles, blog roll, author profile links.

iv. High quality - contextual links, press releases, good directories.

v. The best quality – authority sites with low outbound links, e.g. edu, gov, news sites, home page of a high PR site.

4. Vary The PR Of Your Links

Whilst it may seem tempting to focus only on high quality links, this is not how a natural link profile actually looks.

When a site picks up natural links, it is going to receive a larger number of links from sites with a PR 0 then sites from a PR 5.

The fact is, the Internet has millions more sites with a PR of 0 then it does with a PR 5.

Whichever metric you use to define authority, whether it is PR or page authority/domain authority, make sure to mix up the authority of the links that your site receives.

If you want to strengthen the links coming into your site then you should make an effort to improve the link quality of all of your profiles, for example your social media and web 2.0 accounts.

As your existing links get stronger, the authority of your website will build.

If you are regularly producing quality content and building up the PR of your existing profiles then you can turn your site into a true authority.

This will help you to immunise your site from future algorithm updates.

5. Related Links

The backlink profile of a website that has acquired natural links should have a high percentage of relevant links. These links would come from sites that are either in the same niche or in a closely related niche.

It makes sense for a website in the dog training niche to link to a site about vets. Linking to another site that can provide useful information for your visitors will enhance their browsing experience and help you to build trust with them.

The search engines work in a similar way. They build trust with us, the end user, by making sure that high quality, relevant results are displayed when we type a keyword phrase into the search box.

A website with a high percentage of relevant backlinks gives a signal to the search engines that it has value to users in that niche. This is why a relevant backlink will always hold more weight than a non relevant link.

A website owner that cares about their audience will make an effort to provide information that is useful to them. There would be no logical reason to link out to a site in a different niche unless you were deliberately performing SEO.

There are always exceptions to any rule and Google, as sophisticated as it is, cannot make decisions like a human does.

For this reason, link juice still flows from a non relevant link; it just doesn't carry as much weight as a relevant link would.

Finding links from a relevant site can be a challenge if you are outsourcing your SEO.

It is more expensive to pick up a relevant link in an SEO campaign because there are substantially fewer relevant sites available to an SEO professional than general sites.

A general rule of thumb in SEO is if a link is hard to achieve, it will usually hold more value.

Google analyses the incoming links of a website that is linking out to yours before determining how relevant a link is.

In the past, it was possible to re-theme a property like a web 2.0 site just by changing the On Page content.

If for example you had a web 2.0 site about technology and later changed it to dog training, Google would count the link as relevant.

Today, Google now looks at the incoming backlinks to that web 2.0 site. If the majority of them are related to technology and there are none about dog training this will raise a flag.

Your website will still receive the benefit of the backlink from the web 2.0 site but it may only be counted as partially relevant.

Another factor that Google gives high priority to is geography. A local business website that has authority and age would naturally pick up links from relevant sites and non relevant sites that are in the same geographic location.

In our tests we have found that Google favours links that come from the same country.

If you are running a local SEO campaign then you should attempt to build a mixture of relevant links and links from other businesses in the same city.

6. Permanent Links

Not every link that is built in an SEO campaign will be permanent.

Links can get deleted for a number of reasons: a website owner might carry out a manual review of the blog comments on their site to clear up spam or the website ownership may change hands leading to a re-structure of the content.

If you have built several hundred links to your website over a period of months then you should expect to lose a handful of these over time.

This is natural and is to be expected. If you are carrying out White Hat SEO it is normal for your website to acquire new links too.

If the search engines see that new links are replacing lost ones this is fine. If a website loses a large number of links in a short space of time and your website is young then you may end up with a penalty.

Having a large spike of links built over a 2 or 3 month period and then losing them is a possible signal that you may be paying for links because as soon as you stop paying the links are taken down.

Even if you reach page one after your SEO campaign is finished it is a good idea to carry on building a few links to your website for several weeks or months.

Drip feeding links can help to maintain your rankings.

If you are in a competitive niche then it's likely that some of your competitors will be running SEO campaigns for their websites.

If you don't maintain your link building efforts then you may lose your rankings. Ask your SEO firm for a drip feed maintenance plan once your full campaign has finished.

7. Paid Linking

Google recommends that paid links, for example through banner advertising, are made 'No Follow'.

Paying for a link to transfer Page Rank, i.e. for SEO benefit is against Google's terms of service and can lead to a penalty.

A vendor that sells links usually advertises their service on their website. I strongly recommend that you stay clear of websites that sell links in this manner.

With millions of blogs on the Internet, the reality is that Google and the other search engines cannot police the entire Internet.

However, as the algorithms become more sophisticated there will always be a risk of getting caught. The penalties are severe and may even lead to your site getting de-indexed.

If you are looking at ways to monetise your site and you receive a high volume of traffic then you may want to consider using Google AdSense.

This is a program run by Google to allow website owners to deliver ads on their website.

Ads can be in text, image, video or interactive media format. Google decides the content of the ads based on the niche of the web page. Revenue is generated on a per click or per impression basis.

If your site is new or not ranking highly then having AdSense on your website is not a good idea. Although AdSense is run by Google, using it can negatively impact on your rankings.

Use AdSense if you are already ranking or if your site receives traffic from other sources, independent of the search engines.

8. Choosing The Right Anchor Text

A site that picks up natural links has lots of anchor text variation, for example 'click here', 'check this website', 'go to http://www.site.com' (where site is your domain name) and so on.

It is highly unlikely that your site will pick up a large chunk of links specifically for your main keyword unless your site is an emd. If that's the case then you need to be very careful about over optimisation.

Before Penguin came along it was possible to have a large majority of your anchor text backlinks repeating your main keyword. With each Penguin update, the need to vary your anchor text profile is becoming stricter.

This means that you cannot build the majority of your links with the anchor text 'Dog Training Specialist' if your site is in the dog training niche.

When you initially build links to your site with a new anchor text you will see a rankings boost.

If you don't vary your anchor text up then eventually you will get hit with an over optimisation penalty and your site will take a dip in the rankings.

If you're not sure what keywords to include in your link profile then I recommend that you start with Google's keyword planner and use additional keywords that get monthly search volume.

Long term, sustainable rankings come when you build authority. A site that is truly an authority will cover several keywords in that niche and therefore be optimised for more than just a single phrase.

A mistake that I see many businesses make is in targeting the short tail keywords that account for the highest amount of monthly search volume from Google's keyword planner.

Short tail keywords are harder to rank for because of the higher competition and they may not always provide the return that you are expecting because the traffic is lower quality.

A better strategy is to go after long tail keywords, i.e. search phrases that have several words. If your site is young this can be a really quick way to pick up some profitable returns.

Long tail keywords are referred to as 'low hanging fruit' because they are easier to rank for. Whilst the search volume is much lower, the traffic is more targeted and usually easier to convert.

For example, a person that searches for 'dogs' may only be looking for general information where as the person that is searching for a 'dog training specialist' is more likely to be in need of your services.

Keep in mind that Google's keyword planner tool isn't perfect. It may throw up some random ideas that are not relevant to your niche so you don't have to target every suggestion that it provides.

9. Link Diversity

Authority sites build trust with the search engines by picking up links from a wide variety of sources. In previous years, .edu (University) and .gov (Government) links were the best links to get.

Having a few of these 'golden' links could get you onto the first page, or very close, in most niches.

In 2011, Google devalued the ranking weight that .edu and .gov links carried. Today, .edu and .gov links are still seen as trusted, authority links but their ranking power has diminished and is now on a par with other regular domains.

More recently, social bookmark links were in vogue but as these became easier to access and got spammed, Google also devalued their ranking power.

The dilemma for the search engines is to find ways to reduce spam results in the SERPs but at the same time keep results relevant to end users.

To combat mass efforts to manipulate the search results, Google has aggressively de-indexed a number of blog networks in recent years.

In 2012, Google targeted the popular blog network, Build My Rank. This had a massive effect on many SEO agencies which used Build My Rank to achieve first page rankings for their client websites.

In 2013, the Russian blog network, SAPE, which was commonly used by Black Hat SEOs to get fast rankings, had many of its sites de-indexed.

More recently in 2014, Google turned their attention to guest blog networks. A guest blog network is a platform that allows a user to post an article and acquire a Do Follow link back to their website.

Google hit two of the biggest guest blog networks with manual penalties: MyGuestBlog and PostJoint.

The de-indexing of these networks affected thousands of sites that were using the guest blog networks to acquire links and traffic.

The moral here is to diversify your links using as many different sources as possible. If you rely on only one type of link building then you leave your site vulnerable to future updates.

A good link profile will reduce your risk and keep your rankings strong.

10. Link Location

The location of your links on a web page also plays a big role in determining how much link juice will flow from the source website to yours. The best links to get, for location, are contextual links.

A contextual link is an anchor text link that is created within the main body of an article. This type of link is hard to obtain because only the author (or the website owner) has discretion over what links will go into the content.

By contrast, a link in the comments section carries less weight because they are easier to obtain and can be created by external users.

As with link diversity, it is important to have links that come from a range of different locations.

The big exception is the footer. A few links from the footer are fine but if the majority of your links come from the footer section of other websites, this will raise a flag and likely land you with a penalty.

A few years ago, Black Hat SEOs used the footer section to build mass links through software distribution. Since the footer appears on every page of a website, a link in this section helped the source website to achieve fast rankings.

Google clamped down on this practice with Penguin, declaring the footer section as open to manipulation and therefore to be seen as unnatural if used to acquire mass links.

If you discover that you have a large number of footer links in your backlink profile then you should contact the website owners and ask them to make the footer link to your website into a No Follow.

A diversified link profile will have links from the following locations:

- Contextual Article

- Blogroll (sidebar links)

- Author Bio (usually at the bottom of an article)

- Blog Comments Section

- Profile (e.g. your Twitter bio)

- Footer

- Forum Posts (either within the post or in the user's signature)

- Directories

- Web 2.0

11. Getting Forum Links

An under-rated source of traffic is forum links. Getting a forum link is a manually labour intensive process but the rewards can be high.

Depending on how popular the forum is it is quite possible to drive hundreds, if not thousands, of visitors just from a few quality posts made in the forum.

The art to creating trust in a forum is to avoid spamming the forum with links from the beginning. Doing so will likely get your account suspended or banned by a forum moderator.

If you regularly post for a few weeks or months and create a good reputation for helping other users with their questions and problems, you'll find it easier to drive traffic from the forum back to your website.

Once they are on your website you can promote your products or services to them.

Many forums with high Page Rank also get their pages indexed in the search engines so if you title your post with a keyword that provides an answer to a common problem, you could pick up organic traffic from the search engines to your post.

To find a niche related forum use the following search strings in Google:

"forum" + keyword

allintitle:forum + keyword

A search with "forum" + dog training returns 46.8m results:

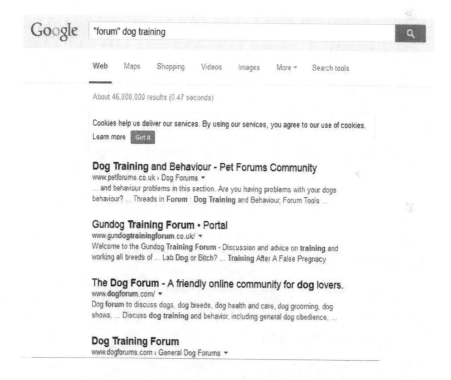

Whereas a search with the second string returns 6.8m results:

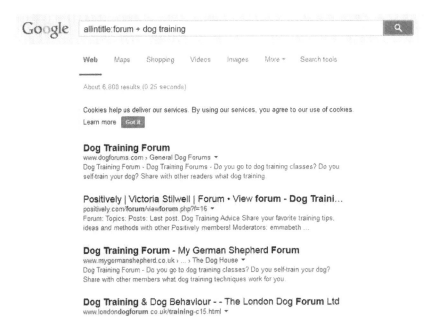

The key difference in the search strings is the targeting.

In a less popular niche you may get decent results with the first search string.

The first example above targets forums that cover dog training but are not specific to just dog training, i.e. they cover other dog topics too.

If you are in a popular niche then you can find more targeted results with the second search string.

In the second example above, we are looking for specific forums that have dog training in the title of the forum and these will be more relevant to our keyword.

Like with any type of link building it is important to vary the platforms from where you acquire your backlinks.

Relying on forum links can be a great way to drive traffic but if the majority of your links all come from the same forum then you will get a diminishing return.

After Penguin, Google devalued multiple links that point to a single property and which come from the same i.p. address.

This means that having links in your posts across different pages on a forum does not provide the same benefit that it used to.

However, you can always include other properties in your posts and your signature, like a YouTube video or a social media profile, to strengthen the power of these pages that point back to your website.

12. Getting Trusted Links

Until 2011, .edu and .gov backlinks were the gold standard of links for SEO.

One of the reasons that Google devalued their ranking power in 2011 was because the blogs that students put up on .edu sites got hammered with spammy comment links.

Today, .edu and .gov links still carry a lot of trust so it is worth adding these to your link profile if the link is relevant, i.e. the student's blog or the Government blog are related to your niche.

The root domain of most educational and Government institutes have a high Page Rank so these links have power by virtue of the domain's authority.

Traditionally, it has been hard to acquire a .gov backlink but times have changed and even Government departments are now using blogs on their web pages.

Finding them is easy once you know what search string to put into Google.

Note that .gov blogs are more formal and heavily moderated so outbound links pointing to external websites will normally be removed. For this reason you may prefer to focus your efforts on .edu blogs.

Try the following search strings in Google:

site:.edu inurl:blog

site:.edu "keyword" "blog posts"

site:.edu "keyword" "post comment"

site:.edu "keyword" "faculty blogs"

site:.edu "keyword" "staff blogs"

site:.edu "keyword" "student blogs"

Tip: Check that the blog has been updated in the last month, either from the post date or from the comments listed underneath the post.

Most comments are manually approved so there is no point in making the effort to create an intelligent comment if the blog has been neglected as the chances of getting your comment approved will be slim.

Commenting on a blog that is in your niche may help the approval rate and will be viewed as a stronger backlink to your site.

13. Other Ways To Get A University Link

If you are a graduate of a University then it's worth asking the alumni office for a link to your website.

Universities are keen to profile the success of their students as it enhances the reputation of the University in the media and can also help to attract new students.

If you own a local business that is close to a University then it's worth asking for a link to your website.

Your service doesn't need to be exclusive to their students but you may want to offer an incentive like a 10% discount on purchases.

Almost any local business owner could benefit from a University link, e.g. restaurants, clothes shops, hair salons, travel agents, gyms etc.

Even a local business that provides professional services, e.g. law firms, accountants and I.T. companies can get a University link by offering internships or summer vacation placements to the students.

Chapter 7 Summary

Key Takeaways

In Chapter 7 you learnt the following:

1. Why it is important to have a natural link building profile.

2. The difference between link types and which to focus on.

3. Acquiring trust with Google through relevant links.

4. How to choose the right anchor text to avoid an over optimisation Penguin penalty.

5. The importance of link diversity: in particular link quality, link location and link source to make your backlink profile look natural to Google.

6. How to boost traffic to your site through forum links.

7. How to get trusted links from .edu sites using search strings in Google.

8. Why it is not worth pursuing a link from a .gov blog.

What To Expect In Chapter 8

In the next chapter we'll learn how to recover rankings from an algorithm update penalty, why Google will de-index a website for persistent flouting of its terms and conditions and what action to take if this occurs.

We'll also cover the links to avoid if you want to stay in Google's good books.

Chapter 8

Recovering From A Penalty

When a site receives natural backlinks there is always a chance that it may acquire links from sites that are considered to be 'bad neighbourhoods'.

If your site has age, authority and a decent amount of quality links (PR0 and above) then Google will ignore a few bad links in your profile.

If however your site is new, with only a few links, and your link profile gets filled with a large majority of links from a bad neighbourhood, your site will likely get hit with a penalty.

A penalty will result in your site taking a big dip in the SERPs. Shake ups in the SERPs can also occur when an algorithm update happens.

If you notice that your site was affected but many of your competitors kept their rankings, you should check in Google Webmaster Tools (GWT).

It is here that you will receive a notice to inform you if you have been hit with a penalty.

If there are no notices in GWT then your dip in rankings is likely down to an automatic algorithm penalty.

It is far easier to recover from an algorithm penalty, by undoing any recent changes to your link profile, than it is to recover from a manual penalty.

If you have received a manual penalty in GWT then I recommend that you seek the help of an SEO professional.

Recovering from a manual penalty can be a long, arduous journey and repairing the damage will involve significant cost. This is not something that you want to be tackling on your own.

Algorithm penalties are far more common and it's possible to sometimes recover from these by just picking up as many quality links as you can.

This will dilute the effect of the bad links that you have acquired and push the percentage ratio of your anchor text back under the threshold that triggered the automatic penalty.

I recommend that you seek the help of an SEO professional to help you analyse your link profile. Carrying on with an existing strategy may exacerbate the problem.

An SEO professional will be able to calculate whether your site has been hit by Penguin, which covers over optimisation on anchor text or whether you have been hit by Panda, which covers poor On Page and duplicate content.

If you discover links pointing to your site that you don't like, the best solution is to contact the website owner and ask them to remove the link.

However this can get tricky if you suddenly discover dozens or even hundreds of links that don't look good.

Contacting an owner is usually as simple as completing the contact form on their website. If there isn't a form available then you can try looking up the registration details of the offending domain by using 'Who Is' tools.

Some website owners install a privacy or 'Who Is' guard protection so if you can't access the website owner through this method, have a look to see if the website owner has any social media profiles.

As a last resort, you can also use Google's 'Disavow Tool' to tell Google to ignore some of the links in your backlink profile.

I mention this as a last resort because using the Disavow Tool can destroy any hard earned 'good links' as well as the 'bad links' if you're not sure what you're doing.

Some of my fellow SEO professionals have told me that even with the Disavow Tool it can still take months to resolve a penalty.

Before you use the tool you should make every effort possible to manually clean up any spammy links that are pointing to your site.

Using Google's Disavow Tool can also lead to a manual review of your website and your backlink history.

Every link that you have built will be under scrutiny so if you have engaged in shady SEO practices in the past, but your site has to date slipped under the radar, then you may want to think hard about taking this action.

If your site has been penalised and also de-indexed but you are confident that you haven't done anything wrong then you may want to consider putting in a manual reconsideration request.

Google takes manual reconsideration requests very seriously and will not reinstate a site that has been de-indexed unless you have taken all appropriate steps to fix your site.

If you don't understand why your site has been hit then you will need to speak with an SEO professional. They should be able to carry out some research and analyse your site to see if it is recoverable.

It may be that your site has just slipped a couple of hundred places and that you are experiencing an over optimisation penalty that can be fixed.

Finally, as gut wrenching as it may sound, it may be easier if you start with a fresh new domain.

To do this, de-index your existing pages by blocking Googlebot in your .htaccess file and then transfer all of your existing content onto a new site with a different hosting provider.

If you are determined to persist with a manual reconsideration request then prepare yourself for a long struggle.

If you do manage to get your penalty removed after several months, you should note that it will be difficult to recover your previous rankings.

Google applies the reset switch on a reinstated domain.

This means starting from scratch and rebuilding all the trust and authority that you acquired over months or years. Your domain will also be monitored more carefully.

If you are in a highly competitive niche then you need to question if you have the patience and the resources to recover your site or whether it would be a better use of your efforts to start with a different domain that has no previous history.

Keep in mind that if you start a new site on the same hosting account and with the same i.p. address as the old penalised site, you may find it much harder to rank the new site.

Google often applies penalties to an i.p. address and not just the domain.

1. Checklist: Links To Avoid

There are no specific platforms like wikis, web 2.0 sites, social bookmarks, etc. that are considered bad and which you should avoid getting a link from.

What you need to do is steer clear of anything that is associated with spam.

For example:

i) Bad neighbourhoods (pharmaceutical 'magic pill', adult and gambling sites).

ii) Low quality article directories. Whilst there are some directories that can help bring fantastic traffic to your site, there are equally many out there that got penalised for being 'spam farms', i.e. producing low quality duplicate content.

   With the search engines cracking down on duplicate content, do you really want to be submitting your article to a hundreds of low quality directories?

iii) Forums. Having a link in the signature of your profile may be good for bringing in new traffic to your site, particularly if you are active on different forums, but it's not going to help with your rankings.

   The link is seen as low quality and spam by the search engines because it is repeated across many pages in that same forum, i.e. every time that you create a new post.

If you want to use forums effectively then consider restricting your link building to only within posts (if allowed), creating multiple personas (be careful as some forums restrict the amount of users on the same i.p. address) or using forums that No Follow your signature links.

iv) Low quality social bookmarking sites (not to be confused with social media platforms). Until recently, these were a favourite of the search engines.

Social bookmarking sites receive a huge amount of traffic and for this reason they still get regularly crawled by the search engines.

However, a large number of links from these sites can negatively impact your rankings if they are from low quality social bookmark sites.

Social bookmark links are easy to acquire and there are many tools to help you pick up free links.

Many social bookmark sites were hit with spam tools so you need to extremely careful if you do use them.

v) Reciprocal Linking. The search engines see this as a deliberate act to manipulate their search results so you're more likely to either lose the benefit of the link or get hit with a penalty.

vi) Paid Linking. Google makes it very clear that paying for links is against their terms of service. In reality it does still happen and this method can be difficult to police. Be very careful if you go down this route.

The search engines know which of the bigger sites offer a paid linking service and if you end up with a link from one of these 'neighbourhoods' then your site will get hit with a penalty.

Relevant Bad Neighbourhood Links

If your site is in a 'bad neighbourhood' niche then getting a backlink from another site in the same 'bad neighbourhood' niche will still count as a relevant link.

However, Google's algorithms are complex so whilst you may receive a temporary boost from this relevant link, it is likely that another part of the algorithm will hit you with an automatic penalty.

In the end you may not receive any benefit from acquiring this relevant link and the likelihood is that you could end up worse off.

My advice is that you steer well clear of pharmaceutical, gambling and adult niches.

Chapter 8 Summary

Key Takeaways

In Chapter 8 you learnt the following:

1. The difference between an algorithm update penalty and a bad neighbourhood link penalty.

2. Action steps for how to remove bad links that point to your website and how to ask Google to ignore links in your backlink profile.

3. What action to take if your website has been de-indexed from the SERPs.

4. A checklist of links to avoid.

What To Expect In Chapter 9

In the next chapter we'll find out how video can boost the traffic back to your website and help you to convert viewers into customers.

You'll learn why video gets more clicks than a regular website in the SERPS.

We'll also cover the top ranking factors in YouTube to help you dominate the biggest video hosting site in the world.

Chapter 9

YouTube Video SEO

YouTube is Google's video hosting platform and has the third highest traffic in the world after Google and Facebook. YouTube videos stand out in the SERPs because they have a thumbnail image attached to them.

You can drive traffic to your website by linking to it in the description part underneath your YouTube video and also by having a call to action within your video.

If your video is educational and adds value to the end user, it is possible to convert viewers into customers with YouTube.

Until 2013, it was very easy to rank a YouTube video on the first page of Google.

The SEO rules that applied to a website could be thrown out of the window for YouTube by virtue of its high domain authority (PR 9).

Many SEO professionals took advantage of this authority and used old style Black Hat tactics, e.g. thousands of links in a short space of time to rank their videos, safe in the knowledge that Google would never de-index a YouTube video.

YouTube does have strict rules, e.g. no commercial videos, but many of their rules are related to matters like copyright infringements and the use of fake profiles to artificially inflate the popularity of a video.

In 2013, Google finally adjusted its algorithm for ranking YouTube videos.

In 2015, it is still possible to get a YouTube video to rank but the SEO strategies need to be closer aligned to the strategies used for ranking a website, particularly in competitive niches.

1. YouTube Ranking Factors

YouTube has several On Page factors that you can take advantage of to help give your videos a boost:

1. Make sure your video is public otherwise it won't get indexed in Google.

2. Include your keyword in the title of the video.

3. Put your main keyword in the video tags along with other related keywords.

4. Have a full description. Don't use just one or two lines in the description. Include a link to your website and use the available space in the description area to its full potential.

    This means treating the description like a blog page: include an article with several hundred words of content underneath the actual video.

    Sprinkle your keywords in the description but don't stuff them in if it looks unnatural.

5. Share your video on social media platforms like Facebook and Twitter to help get organic views and social likes.

   Do not purchase views for your video. This is a Black Hat tactic.

   YouTube's algorithms have become increasingly sensitive to views from bots (i.e. machine-generated views which are not from real humans).

   Any attempts to use a fake profile to increase the popularity of the video will result in an infringement notice.

   Your video will be removed if you engage in this practice and your account may get suspended with repeated violations.

6. Comments on your video (delete any spammy looking comments). Encourage your users to leave a comment below the video. You can do this by including a call to action in your video or in the description area.

7. Shares (e.g. in social media posts), likes and subscribers to the video provide a ranking boost.

8. Embed your video into your website and preferably on a web page with authority, e.g. the home page.

   This can be done by clicking on the embed button underneath the YouTube video and pasting the <iframe> ... </iframe> code into a post/page on your website.

9. Closed captions -> if your video has speech then YouTube will automatically transcribe the voice and convert it into a file called 'closed captions'.

   Since YouTube's automatic transcription service is machine generated, it is poor and at times, comical.

   You can download the closed captions file by going into the 'Advanced Settings' and saving the closed captions file to your desktop.

   Edit this file in notepad and correct any spelling errors, especially your keywords.

   Be sure to keep the file ending as .sbv as YouTube will not accept the default .txt ending that notepad saves in.

10. Geo targeting: In the 'Video Manager' section find the 'Advanced Settings' tab for your video and then click on the search button next to the 'Video location' tab.

    YouTube will offer you the maps service.

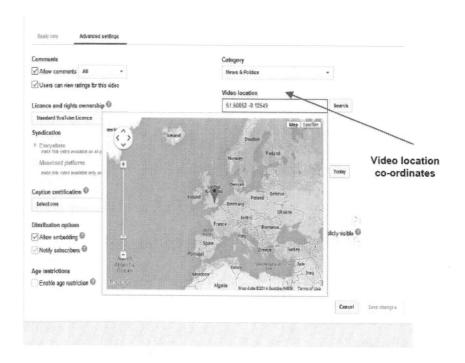

Drag the red pointer towards the geographic location of where the video should be targeted for. This is useful if you have a business with a fixed location.

If you are in a low to medium competition niche then you may find that your YouTube video ranks with just On Page SEO.

Optimising the above factors will certainly help your video to rank highly for your keyword in YouTube's own search engine.

To get your video ranking higher in Google you can start an Off Page SEO campaign by building backlinks to it in the same manner as you would for a regular website.

Chapter 9 Summary

Key Takeaways

In Chapter 9 you learnt the following:

1. How to convert viewers into customers with video marketing.

2. Why videos stand out in the SERPs.

3. How to avoid getting your YouTube video and account suspended.

4. How to optimise your video to get it ranking in both YouTube and Google.

What To Expect In Chapter 10

In the next chapter we'll find out which ranking factors give you the biggest oomph, why Google is going social and what tools you can use to measure the authority of any website on the Internet.

We'll also cover the other top ranking factors that Google uses in its algorithm so that you understand where to focus your efforts.

Chapter 10

The Top Ranking Factors In SEO Today

The top four ranking factors in SEO today are:

1. User Signals

2. Relevant Terms

3. Social Signals

4. Backlinks

As the Internet evolves and becomes more social, Google has begun to rely heavily on user signals to determine what content should rank at the top of the SERPs.

User signals include factors like click through rate, a low bounce rate and time on site. User signals are influenced by relevant terms, which is your On Page content.

If the content is relevant to the end user they will stay on the site for longer and click through to other pages. If the content isn't relevant, the user will instead hit the back button in their browser and return to Google to extend their search.

Social signals are the likes, shares, votes, pins, or views people place on Facebook, Twitter and other social media sites that filter out to the search engines.

Social signals indicate that your brand is being talked about by consumers, and this improves your SERP ranking because search engines view social signals as trusted recommendations.

As social media continues to grow, people are visiting websites based on recommendations from their friends, either directly or through social signals.

Sharing a link, e.g. a YouTube video on Facebook, counts as a social signal to that YouTube video.

The algorithm for social signals is currently in its infancy. This means that all users of a particular social media platform carry the same authority, irrespective of how many 'fans' or 'followers' they have.

The key factor is which social media platform to use and this is discussed below.

The importance of backlinks has gradually fallen but is still a critical factor for sustainable rankings. Google understands that many companies employ SEO agencies to artificially manipulate their SERP ranking.

The high precedence given to backlinks in previous years allowed websites to rank at the top of the SERPs even if they did not provide the best user experience.

By giving priority to user signals, Google is attempting to make the SERPs look more natural. If a topic is trending, it will be the users that determine how high a website ranks compared to its competitors.

A user is influenced by the content on a website: if the content is good they will stay on the site for longer.

1. User Signals

The most important of these is click through rate. Google is a piece of software and cannot understand human emotions. Instead, it relies on what other users are clicking through on to determine relevance and importance.

Our research has shown that click through rate is more important to sites that are already on the front page of the SERPs. The majority of users never go past the first page of results.

If your website is on the second page or further back, you should focus on creating regular, quality content and marketing your content across different social platforms.

Quality content will make your website sticky and help to increase your conversion rates, whether that is an opt-in to your newsletter or achieving a social share for your content.

2. Relevant Terms

Good content will naturally include words or phrases that Google defines as 'co-occurrent'. Co-occurrence is the inclusion of related terms, or synonyms, in the context of your article.

A longer article will encourage a user to stay on your website for longer if they find your content relevant to what they are searching for.

Adding media like images and video will help to engage the user and reinforce to the search engines that your site is relevant.

3. Social Signals

The social networks that provide the biggest ranking boost are:

I.   Google Plus: shares and posts

II.   Facebook: shares, comments and likes

III.   Pinterest: through re pins

IV.   Twitter: through re tweets

LinkedIn, Stumble Upon, Instagram and other social networks like Tumblr and MySpace carry some weight but not as much as the 'big 4' above.

4. Quality Backlinks

I.   Page Rank of the backlink (on a scale of 0-10 where 0 is the lowest and 10 is the highest).

Page Rank is an indication of how much authority and trust is placed on a website by the search engines.

Google currently favours older domains with a good history (i.e. one that has not been penalised through Black Hat SEO) over a new registered site that has no history.

A website builds authority and trust by adding value to its readers. This can be achieved by producing regular content and having people either share the content on social networking sites or link to it from their own websites.

Note: Page Rank also has an influence on social networks and the ranking boost that a social signal from these networks provides.

The 'big 4' social networks currently have a Page Rank of 8 or above.

II.   Number of backlinks (with Page Rank)

- A backlink from a site with a Page Rank of 9 will carry significantly more weight than 10 backlinks from a site with a Page Rank of 0.

  You should focus on picking up backlinks from sites that have a minimum Page Rank of 1.

III.   Relevancy of the backlink

- If you are in the law niche, a backlink from a law/business related website will carry much more weight than a backlink from a technology website (Page Rank being equal).

Since 2013, Google has been playing down the importance of Page Rank as a measure of authority.

Many SEO professionals believe that Google maintains its own internal Page Rank score but does not release this information to the public.

The absence of regular public updates to the Page Rank toolbar has made authority harder to evaluate.

To assess the quality of a backlink you should now analyse the score allocated by Moz: DA (Domain Authority) and PA (Page Authority) and by Majestic SEO (Trust Flow and Citation Flow) and see if these match up to the Page Rank.

If in doubt, consult an SEO professional.

5. Do I Need Social Media?

You may be wondering if it's worth hiring a social media expert, given the importance that social media has in SEO today.

If you have a budget, I recommend that you have someone create and update a Facebook fan page, create and regularly post onto a business Twitter account and also share your content on Google Plus.

Social media may not give you an immediate return on your investment and it may be hard for you to track results with it, but if you use it consistently and engage with your audience then it can help to build your brand.

If you are a local business owner, on a limited budget, you can use tools like HootSuite to schedule your posts across different social media platforms.

This means that you can focus on your business during working hours and plug all your content into the platform in the evening to be published the following day.

Consider: It's highly likely that most of your competition hasn't figured out how to use social media effectively.

Sure, they may have jumped on the bandwagon a couple of years ago when social media was the new craze, but chances are they gave up within a few months after failing to get a return on their investment.

Some niches, e.g. professional service providers like plumbers, lawyers and accountants, might be better focussing on social platforms that are geared more to business, e.g. LinkedIn.

6. Social Signals Decay

Yes you read that right. Many SEO professionals aren't even aware of this. Although social signals contribute a large ranking factor to your SEO campaign, the effectiveness of these signals wears off as time passes.

Stop for a minute and think about this. Google doesn't like SEO (which ultimately is manipulation of its search engine rankings).

If you watch any videos on YouTube about SEO, it actively encourages you to get 'natural links' through your marketing efforts.

The fact is, news changes on a daily basis so what is of interest today will be replaced with something different tomorrow.

The same applies to your social networking sites.

Most people aren't interested in what happened a few weeks back. They're only interested in what's going on today.

If you have a community of fans built up, e.g. likes to your Facebook fan page, a large number of followers on Twitter or Google Plus or even an email list of subscribers to a newsletter, then as long as you're posting content - whether it be to your website or one of your social network pages - you can maintain the importance of your social signals.

But if your competition is local and your fellow business owners don't have deep pockets, do you need to spend money on a social media campaign if they aren't either?

7. Build Authority To Your Site

"Google likes to behave like a news channel".

If you want to maintain your authority and your rankings, you should be posting content to your website and also to your social network sites at least a couple of times every month. If your site is new then you should aim to post content at least once a week.

i. What If I Want To Post More Frequently?

There's no problem with posting content to your site on a daily basis. But if your site is new then you need to build up trust in Google's eyes and this doesn't happen overnight.

If you're confident that you'll able to maintain posting new content regularly, both to your website and your social media profiles, then go for it. Online newspaper sites post several times a day and have Google's bot crawling their site for regular updates.

The more quality content you can produce and the more backlinks and social signals you acquire to each piece of your content, the quicker you will be able to build authority with Google.

A lot of website owners get excited when they first launch their website and they make an effort to post regularly. After a few weeks or months they burn out and stop updating their site.

This behaviour doesn't look natural to Google and if you stop building authority, particularly in the early months, you may see your site drop in rankings.

If your competitors have a large number of indexed pages then you'll need to play catch up by producing quality content on a regular basis and getting your content syndicated across the Internet.

If you need ideas about what to write about, you can begin by answering the frequently asked questions from your existing customers.

You can also look at what is trending in your industry and put your own spin on it. This can be a great way to leverage existing traffic and siphon it to your own website.

The search engines are not looking for original ideas but for original content instead. The more quality content you have, the easier it will be to build authority for your website.

ii. Slow And Steady Wins The Race

The same analogy applies with SEO link building campaigns. Slow and steady wins the race.

If an SEO company promises you page one rankings within a matter of days, and you know that you have medium to high competition in your industry, give them a wide berth.

Chances are that they've figured out a temporary loophole in the algorithm through a Black Hat technique.

They may well get you to page one but Google always closes all Black Hat loopholes eventually.

Your ranking will be short lived and the likelihood is that you'll end up with a penalty and loss of earnings along with it.

8. Backlinks Are Still King

Let's go back and consider the other big ranking factors in Off Page SEO: social signals and quality backlinks. You've learned that social signals decay over time.

However, a backlink from another website will stick until either it gets manually removed or the website is no longer hosted online.

A backlink therefore doesn't decay over time like a social signal does.

For this reason, quality backlinks are still considered to be the ultimate vote of confidence by Google.

Google is a bot: it cannot differentiate between high quality content and decent quality content like human beings can.

Google therefore relies on user signals and how many quality links are pointing to a website as an indication of how high it should rank.

Google can however detect when content is duplicated or poorly written, e.g. spelling errors and grammatical mistakes.

The algorithm uses the number of links pointing to the root domain as well as the number of links that point to the inner page of the website where the post is.

This is why new content from authority sites like Amazon or Wikipedia often ranks high even without any backlinks to the actual post.

Social signals will give your website a short term boost but if you can't maintain your social campaigns then there's little point in you focussing your efforts on social media.

However, this doesn't mean that social signals are a waste of time. If you want to rank for the long term then you need to give Google what it's looking for, which is natural looking links coming from a wide variety of places.

This means picking up links both from websites and also from social networks.

If you are becoming an authority in your niche then it's only natural that people will start talking about you and sharing your posts across networks like Facebook, Twitter and Google Plus.

Owners of other websites will start linking to content on your website and your existing customers may rave about how good a service you provided for them on their Facebook account.

Google and the other major search engines, Bing and Yahoo, pick up on these signals.

9. The Other Ranking Factors

The chart on the following page was compiled by Search Metrics. It shows the ranking factors that Search Metrics discovered as carrying the most weight in Google's algorithm. The results for the top eight ranking factors in Search Metrics' chart tally with our own research.

For the remaining ranking factors, in particular the On Page SEO factors, our results show some small differences to what Search Metrics discovered.

For the purpose of research, I attribute these differences to the way in which we set up our On Page SEO and also to other differences such as:

i.   The age of the domain

ii. Domain authority

iii. Anchor text percentage variation

In summary, our results with Off Page SEO were very similar to the results from Search Metrics but our results with On Page SEO show some differences.

- Search Metrics Chart → Overleaf –

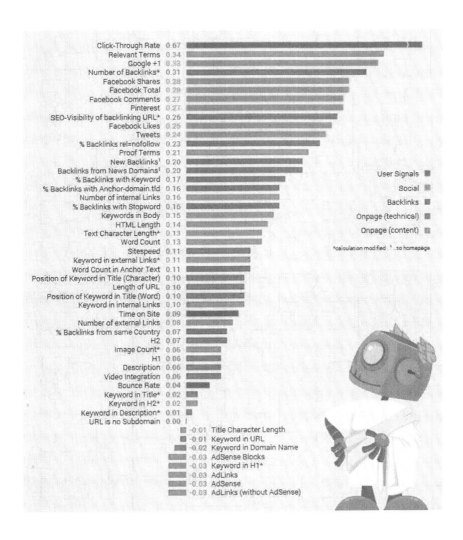

Click-Through Rate	0.67
Relevant Terms	0.34
Google +1	0.33
Number of Backlinks*	0.31
Facebook Shares	0.28
Facebook Total	0.28
Facebook Comments	0.27
Pinterest	0.27
SEO-Visibility of backlinking URL*	0.26
Facebook Likes	0.25
Tweets	0.24
% Backlinks rel=nofollow	0.23
Proof Terms	0.21
New Backlinks[1]	0.20
Backlinks from News Domains[1]	0.20
% Backlinks with Keyword	0.17
% Backlinks with Anchor-domain.tld	0.16
Number of internal Links	0.16
% Backlinks with Stopword	0.16
Keywords in Body	0.15
HTML Length	0.14
Text Character Length*	0.13
Word Count	0.13
Sitespeed	0.11
Keyword in external Links*	0.11
Word Count in Anchor Text	0.11
Position of Keyword in Title (Character)	0.10
Length of URL	0.10
Position of Keyword in Title (Word)	0.10
Keyword in internal Links	0.10
Time on Site	0.09
Number of external Links	0.08
% Backlinks from same Country	0.07
H2	0.07
Image Count*	0.06
H1	0.06
Description	0.06
Video Integration	0.06
Bounce Rate	0.04
Keyword in Title*	0.02
Keyword in H2*	0.02
Keyword in Description*	0.01
URL is no Subdomain	0.00

User Signals
Social
Backlinks
Onpage (technical)
Onpage (content)

*calculation modified [1] ..to homepage

-0.01	Title Character Length
-0.01	Keyword in URL
-0.02	Keyword in Domain Name
-0.03	AdSense Blocks
-0.03	Keyword in H1*
-0.03	AdLinks
-0.03	AdSense
-0.03	AdLinks (without AdSense)

Infographic available at:

http://www.searchmetrics.com/wp-content/uploads/infographic-seo-ranking-factors-2014.jpg

10. Building Your SEO Foundation

Keep in mind that search engines are just software and are programmed to return results using an algorithm.

The search engines use 'spiders' that crawl a website and return this information to a central computer which then processes the information to compile results for an end user.

The spiders do not distinguish between how good looking a site is, what font you use or the colour of your text.

What they are looking for is specific pieces of information to determine what your site is about and who it is relevant for.

This information is shown in the Search Metrics chart, which displays a total of 51 ranking factors.

The first 43 ranking factors are positive ranking factors and the final 8 are factors that provide a negative influence on a website's ranking.

You don't need to focus on every single On Page SEO factor unless you like to get seriously geeky.

What you should do is optimise your website with engaging, quality content to encourage users to stay on your site for longer and help the search engines identify what niche you are in.

This will help you to rank for relevant keyword phrases that your target audience are typing into the search box when they need information.

If you're not sure about what keywords to go after, Google has a great tool called the Keyword Planner. The tool is free to use but I highly recommend that you speak to an SEO professional to help you get the best out of it.

To access the tool just enter 'Keyword Planner' into Google's search box and it will display the tool as the first result. You'll need to login with a Google account (e.g. Gmail) to access the Keyword Planner tool.

On Page SEO is about making sure that you provide relevant information to not just the search engines but also to your end users.

Visitors don't want to hear only about your products and services; they want to know how it will benefit them.

Make your content easy to read by breaking it up into chunks. Do not keyword stuff by repeating your keyword phrases several times in your articles.

SEO professionals engaged in this practice many years ago because it used to work but today it's no longer necessary.

Your keyword only needs to appear once on the page and no more than a handful of times in the same article.

Google's algorithm will figure out what keywords you should rank for through your Off Page SEO efforts.

In summary, good On Page SEO will provide your website with a strong foundation. Do not attempt to over optimise your On Page SEO because you could end up with a penalty.

The websites that reach page one and manage to stay do so because they have built a brand over a sustained period of time.

If you want long term, stable rankings in Google then you need to do the same. Build your brand and your authority by staying consistent with your marketing efforts.

If you need help it's better to speak to an SEO professional rather than guess.

Chapter 10 Summary

Key Takeaways

In Chapter 10 you learnt the following:

1. The four biggest ranking factors today.

2. Tools for measuring the authority of a backlink.

3. If you should jump on the social media bandwagon.

4. Why backlinks are the ultimate vote of confidence for sustained rankings.

5. A list of the main ranking factors that contribute to your website's position in the SERPs.

6. How Google's Keyword Planner tool can help you to find related keyword ideas.

Congratulations, you've reached the end of the training!

I hope you feel energised with all of the knowledge that you've acquired. With the strategies that you've learnt in this book you should feel confident to take action and start dominating your niche online.

I hope you've enjoyed reading this book as much as I have enjoyed sharing my knowledge with you. If you'd like to continue this journey with me then be sure to read the next section.

Next Action Steps

SEO Service London offers a choice of SEO packages to build your business and help you acquire greater visibility online.

If you'd like to know more about SEO or the packages on offer then I invite you to call me on 020 8938 3645 and arrange a consultation. I freely confess to being an SEO geek and would be happy to go all technical with you.

If you decide to go with someone else's services then I urge you to study the top ranking factors in Chapter 10 and ask your SEO professional about them.

Although individually they may not make a huge difference to your SEO campaign, collectively they could be the difference between you making page one or being stuck on page two where hardly anyone will find you.

A good SEO professional will be able to explain what all these ranking factors mean.

If you see their eyes glaze over when you 'talk technical' then you'll know that they're likely selling you a service that is being outsourced to another company.

And if that's the case then you need to ask yourself:

1. Are you getting charged more than you need to?

2. Will the person selling you the SEO service be able to correct something in the SEO campaign if anything goes wrong or if Google makes an algorithm update?

I hope this book has helped you to learn more about SEO.

My aim was to equip you with the knowledge on what's working today.

This will help you to make an informed decision about whether to do your own SEO or whether to hire a professional.

Choosing the wrong SEO may not only be an expensive loss, it could also permanently damage your rankings.

Free Bonus Reminder

Before you go, did you pick up your free bonuses? If you didn't, download them from the link below.

The Audio Book and the Cheat Sheets guide are my gift to you, **100%** FREE.

Download your bonuses from:

http://www.SamAdodra.com/audio-book

Support

If you have any questions contact support:

Email: info@seoservicelondon.org

Tel: +44 (0) 20 8938 3645

I'm interested in the success of my students and would love to hear from you or how you are getting along with your SEO campaigns. Let me know if you picked up any 'Aha!' moments or golden nuggets of information in this book.

Review

If you enjoyed reading this book and feel that you got value from the written book, the Audio version and the Cheat Sheets action guide then kindly leave a review of the book on Amazon.

Short Link: tinyurl.com/SeoBookReview

If the book did not meet your expectations or you do not feel that it's worth a 5 Star Review then please help me to improve it by contacting support.

About The Author

Who Is Sam Adodra?

Sam is a self confessed SEO geek, author, public speaker and digital marketing consultant.

He found his way into marketing whilst studying for an MBA in London, U.K. and realised that he could combine his passion for tech, entrepreneurship and marketing by making a space in the online world.

In his down time, Sam enjoys playing sports, eating fine chocolate and spending time with his family and friends.

If you'd like to connect with Sam you can find him here:

LinkedIn: SamAdodra
http://www.linkedin.com/in/SamAdodra

Facebook: SamAdodra
https://www.facebook.com/SamAdodra

Twitter: @SamAdodra
https://twitter.com/SamAdodra

Glossary

Algorithm

The proprietary processes that search engines use to find and display the most relevant information in relation to a user's search query.

Alt Tags

Short snippets of code that allow you to tag an image photo on your website with short text. The alt tag helps the search engines to interpret the image.

Analytics

The process of tracking website data to determine how well a website is performing. There are a number of software programs that provide analytic functions. One of them is Google Analytics.

Metrics include how long a user stays on a website, how many times a web page is viewed and whether a user clicks through to another page on the website.

Anchor Text

This is the text on a webpage, usually blue in colour, which links out to another website or web page:

<a href="http://www.site.com">Anchor Text</a>

Articles

Text documents that form content on a web page. Normal length is between 300-1000 words. A good article will contain original useful content that relates to the topic of the page.

The search engines read the content on each page and pick out keyword phrases to help interpret what the page is about.

Having content on a web page provides an opportunity to help rank that page for multiple keyword phrases.

Article Syndication

The process of distributing articles across a wide number of platforms including directories, privately owned sites, rich media sites (containing audio, image, pdf, video) and web 2.0 sites to provide a variety of links across different i.p. addresses.

Backlink Boosting

This is a process where the backlinks of a website are collected, then pinged and submitted through RSS feeds and to social bookmarking posts.

This provides a second tier of link building which not only helps to index the first tier of links faster but also provides a boost in power to the first tier of links. This helps the target web page to rank higher.

Black Hat SEO

Any attempt to exploit a loophole in the algorithm to cheat your way to the top. Usually involves shortcuts and manipulation of a website.

Black Hat SEO is prohibited by the search engines and will likely result in a penalty and possible de-indexing (removal) of the website from the search results.

The major search engines each have their own terms of service to help users stay within recommended guidelines.

Most Black Hat techniques no longer work because of filters placed into the algorithm of each major search engine.

Bookmarking

Social bookmarking sites, like Reddit, Digg and StumbleUpon are sites where it is possible to share popular content with other users around the world. The search engines like to know what is popular and will often follow the links placed on social bookmarking sites.

Bounce Rate

This is the number of times that a user lands on a website without clicking through to another page on the website. Bounce rate and the length of time that a user stays on a web page can be measured using analytics software.

Crawling

The process of capturing information on a website by spiders, which are small automated programs run by the search engines. The spiders read through the content on a website and analyse the website structure.

The search engine bot (robot) then assimilates this information, including the number of links and all other ranking factors in the algorithm, to create the search engine results pages (SERPs).

CTR

This is an abbreviation for 'Click Through Rate'.

Do Follow

The tag placed around html code that informs the search engines that link juice (authority) can be passed on to the corresponding web page or website.

Google AdSense

A program run by Google that allows publishers to display authorised ads on their website and get paid every time that someone clicks on the link in that ad.

The publisher must sign up to the Google Network of content sites and give permission for text, image, video, or interactive media advertisements to be shown.

Google reads the content on the page and displays ads that are targeted both to the site content and to the site's audience.

Google Dance

This refers to the large variation in search results that occurs when Google is deciding upon where to place a website in its search results. A website may drop several hundred places and temporarily disappear from the SERPs.

The 'dance' is normally triggered when On Page SEO changes are made, for example to the title of a website, or when new links are built to a website. The variation usually levels off within a few weeks.

Header Tags

These are html code tags denoted by <h1>, <h2>, <h3> and so on. Header tags make the text bigger and stand out and should be reserved for titles and subtitles within an article. The search engines give priority to the header tags so it can be useful to include keywords within the header tags where possible.

HTML

This stands for hypertext markup language. It is the web standard of code to help tag text files, change font size, change colour, include images and create links to other web pages.

Image Alt

A tag that can be added to a picture on a website to help identify to the search engines, and the visually impaired, what the image is about.

Indexing

The process used by the search engines to crawl the web, scan web pages and store information about these web pages to help return relevant search results for end users.

Internal Links

This is a link that sends a visitor to another page or section of the same website.

Keywords

Keywords or key phrases are what a user types into the search box to produce relevant search engine results. The websites that appear on the front page of the search results usually get the bulk of the traffic.

Good On Page SEO includes naming the page url and the page title with the keyword (or synonyms of that keyword) that you want to get found for and then writing relevant content on the page.

The content should be based upon the topic of the keyword. It is usually easier to rank for longer phrases (also referred to as 'long tail keywords') as these bring in more targeted buyers. Short keyword phrases pull in more visitors that are browsing for general information.

Keyword Density

This is the number of times that a keyword phrase is mentioned on a web page.

Keyword Stuffing

This is the process of repeating a keyword numerous times on a web page to try and gain a ranking benefit. It is common for the keyword to sound unnatural in the context of the written content.

Keyword stuffing used to provide an On Page SEO benefit several years ago but it is now more likely to land you with an over optimisation penalty. You should write content for your readers not the search engines.

Links

This is a process of connecting two web pages on the same site (referred to as an internal link) or two different websites together (referred to as an external link) through html code. When a user clicks on the link they are taken to a different url.

Link Building

This is the process of generating inbound links from other websites to a target website.

Link Juice

This is the flow of authority from one website to another and the subsequent benefits that follow, for example Page Rank, Trust Flow and an increase in rankings.

Long Tail

These are keywords that contain several words and are also referred to as search phrases that a user types into the search engines. If "dog" is the head keyword, the tail could be "training specialist" or "tips and tricks" for example.

The long tail keyword would then be "dog training specialist" or "dog tips and tricks". Long tail variations can include millions of related keywords.

Meta Description

The part of the head section of an html page where a summary or description of the web page content can be entered.

The search engines pay close attention to the words in the description and display these words in the SERPs underneath your website url.

An eye catching description can help your website to stand out in the SERPs and increase the click through rate.

Meta Keywords

On the head section of each html page there is a tag where it is possible to enter keywords. This section used to be a ranking factor several years ago but is now largely ignored by the search engines because of the potential to keyword stuff.

No Follow

The tag that is placed in HTML code around a link to inform the search engines that no link juice should be passed on when the link is followed.

Off Page SEO

Off Page optimisation is everything that occurs away from your website to help the search engines pay more attention to it.

This means sharing across different social networks, like Google Plus, Twitter and Facebook, and building backlinks that point to your website with the appropriate anchor text.

A backlink is an indication that your website is more popular. In recent years, the goal used to be to get as many backlinks as possible.

The aim now is to get as many relevant links from authority websites and from a variety of sources so that your link profile looks as natural as possible.

On Page SEO

On Page optimisation refers to the factors on your website that you can change, for example the header tags, use of media, using original content.

PDF Distribution

Sites with high authority like Scribd, Slideshare and Docstoc are places where you can distribute your content. Create a PDF document by gathering your articles and images and then post onto these PDF sharing sites.

You can get a valuable backlink and also increase the amount of targeted traffic to your website.

Pinging

The process of notifying the search engines that a new web url, or update to an existing url, has been made. Pinging can help speed up crawl rates.

PPC

Short for Pay Per Click. This is a method of paying to have an advertisement (ad) displayed and only paying when someone clicks on your advertisement.

There are a number of different platforms across the Internet that offer advertising on a pay per click basis, for example Google, Bing, Facebook, Twitter and LinkedIn.

The major search engines provide ads at the top of their search results. Google's PPC model is called AdWords. If you wish to promote a video on YouTube you can also do so through AdWords. Bing's PPC model is called AdCenter.

Press Release

A press release is a means of sharing a newsworthy story across different media platforms.

Premium press release distribution sites include PR Web and Newswire. A press release can generate a large amount of backlinks to a website and give it a rankings boost if the content is of interest.

Premium press releases are expensive but if done well can enable your content to get picked up and syndicated across hundreds or thousands of different sites, leading to a huge surge in traffic to your website.

Another benefit of a press release is the increased amount of publicity and exposure. The bigger corporations use press releases on a regular basis to help with their marketing.

Re-Written/Spinning Articles

Also referred to as 'spun' content, spinning is a means of replacing words in an article with synonyms or paraphrasing words and sentences to create a unique article.

The purpose is to produce content of the same meaning that can be mass syndicated but which avoids duplicate content penalties from the search engines.

Spun content can be produced either by software or by manually re-writing articles. The quality of readable content produced by spinning software is often dubious so care should be exercised if this route is chosen.

Rich Snippets

A snippet is a sample of content that is shown to a user in the search results, e.g. the text that appears in the description section underneath the url in the SERPs.

A rich snippet is a type of mark up that uses one of the following data formats to enhance how a url appears in the SERPs:

  a. Microdata

  b. Microformats

  c. RDFa

Google recommends using Microdata and more information about how to use this is available from the schema.org website.

There are several benefits in using rich snippets but they all provide the same function, which is to help a url stand out in the SERPs.

Two of the most popular benefits that search engine marketers use rich snippets for are the review ratings, i.e. gold stars, that appear underneath a url or the thumbnail image that appears next to the description of that url.

Using rich snippets can help a website to increase its visibility and attract more clicks.

RSS Syndication

Short for rich site summary but also referred to as really simple syndication. RSS is a standard of web feed that helps a subscriber of a website get informed when an update occurs, for example when there is a new blog entry.

The benefit lies in receiving timely updates or aggregating data from many sites. RSS feeds enable publishers to syndicate data automatically.

The SEO benefit of RSS feeds comes when a number of feeds are mashed up together with feeds from other websites to create extra backlinks.

This can be done by taking the RSS feed of your website and combining it, for example, with feeds from your web 2.0 profiles where you also post content to.

The combined feed is then distributed to feed distribution sites like Feedage or Feedburner, where it can get syndicated to multiple different platforms across the Internet resulting in additional backlinks to each site that has the RSS feed.

Search Query

This is the keyword or phrase that a user types into a search engine.

SEM (Search Engine Marketing)

This refers to all aspects of search, including both organic and paid listings.

SEO (Search Engine Optimisation)

The process of optimising your website's content so it is easy for the search engines to find your content, index it, and determine how relevant it is to a specific search query.

SERPs

This is an abbreviation for 'Search Engine Result Pages'.

Text Links From Websites

When one website links to another a blue text hyperlink is created. The text that is in this link tells the search engines what the corresponding website is about.

It is common for a website linking out to use generic text in the blue hyperlink, for example 'click here' or 'visit this site'.

On other occasions, the text will be the naked url, e.g. http://www.site.com or just simply site.com. Since this is the most common type of link pattern, getting a link like this is seen as a 'natural link'.

In previous years it was possible to have a high percentage of backlinks with the keyword that you wanted to rank for as the anchor text.

Sites with an unnaturally high anchor text link profile were usually those that engaged in SEO.

Google introduced Penguin in 2012 to deal with over optimisation of anchor text backlinks from SEO professionals.

The algorithms of the major search engines are sophisticated and it is now no longer necessary to create a link profile with an artificially high percentage of backlinks containing the keyword that you want to rank for.

Google is able to determine what your website is about by looking at the On Page content and also by analysing the sites that are linking back to you.

This is where the power of relevant links comes into play. If your site is about dog training and you get a link from another dog training site, this is seen as a relevant link.

TLD

This is short for Top Level Domain and is the extension at the end of a domain, e.g. .com or .net or .org.

The demand for additional top level domains has rapidly increased as the number of people accessing the Internet around the world has grown in recent years.

URL

This is short for Uniform Resource Locator and is the series of characters in the address bar of a browser that leads to a web page.

Video Distribution

Creating a video on sites like YouTube, Vimeo and DailyMotion can help you to reach a large audience and drive traffic back to your main website. Like with the web 2.0 sites, each video sharing site has its own rules.

YouTube, which is owned by Google, for example does not allow commercial videos to be hosted on its platform.

 You can however post educational content about your product or service and direct visitors back to your website in this manner.

Like the web 2.0 sites, video sharing sites have high authority in Google. It can be easier to rank a new video than to rank a new website. Another benefit of creating a video is the thumbnail image that shows up in the SERPs.

This can make it easier to attract more clicks and in turn drive more organic traffic back to your website.

Web 2.0 Profiles

A web 2.0 property is a site where users can create a profile, usually a sub domain, and post content on a particular topic as if it were their own blog.

The key difference between a web 2.0 property and creating a blog on your own website is the hosting.

On a web 2.0 property, for example Squidoo, LiveJournal or Weebly, you are creating a profile on someone else's platform and will need to abide by their rules.

There are several advantages to creating a profile on a web 2.0 property.

These include avoiding any hosting costs, the ability to take advantage of the domain's authority to create trust in the search engines for your own sub domain and the ability to promote your profile to other users that also have profiles on that web 2.0 property.

All of these factors can help drive traffic back to your main website.

It is possible to create a powerful backlink from the web 2.0 profile to your main site (or any other url) if you build up the authority of your web 2.0 profile.